EVERY DAY IS A GIFT

"This is the day the Lord has made;
let us be glad and rejoice in it."

—Ps 118:24

EVERY DAY IS A GIFT

MINUTE MEDITATIONS FOR EVERY DAY
TAKEN FROM THE HOLY BIBLE AND
THE WRITINGS OF THE SAINTS

———

Introduction by
Rev. Frederick Schroeder

———

Illustrated

CATHOLIC BOOK PUBLISHING CO.
New York

CONTENTS

NIHIL OBSTAT: Daniel V. Flynn, J.C.D.
Censor Librorum

IMPRIMATUR: ✠ Joseph T. O'Keefe, D.D.
Administrator, Archdiocese of New York

(T-195)

INTRODUCTION

"Now we watch for the DAY hoping that the salvation promised us will be ours when Christ will come again in his glory" (Advent Preface 1).

*E*VERY day is a gift of God for every person. For the Christian, especially for one who prays, each day is special. What makes this so is that Christian faith sustained by prayer reveals a whole new dimension to any and every day. If one believes that and acts on it, as a praying Christian does, it is prayer that puts that person in touch with the spiritual world. This is the invisible world of union with God with the Risen Jesus Christ, one also with our brothers and sisters, one even with the Saints already living in the eternal day (heaven).

What makes a day more fruitful, more meaningful, and so much happier for the person who prays? The answer is Jesus. It is He who brings joy and peace to the life of the person who prays.

A short look at each of the traditional sources of these "Minute Meditations" points out how rich our prayer life becomes if we anchor it not only in our own words but in the words of God. The word of God is presented to us to make God Himself present to us. God's word comes to us in the sayings of Jesus, in the words of people like Paul, Peter, Solomon, Isaiah, and other Prophets, Psalm writers and Wisdom books. This in itself points to a time span that began from the first day, one might say, when God spoke to human beings or when they became aware of God's speaking to them, and that will not end until the last day. Indeed, it will not really end even then because God's word is eternal ("Heaven and earth will pass away but my words will never pass away").

This awareness of the power of prayer—each day prayed and lived in the way God wants it—begins the eternal day, or in a sense anticipates and makes present herein the eternal day. This is so for a number of reasons. Praying these prayers joins us with the Saints who prayed some of these prayers while they were on earth. Praying and meditating on some of these same Scriptures, Psalm prayers, and sayings of the great ones joins us with those who went before us and who are singing God's praises in heaven now.

This points up a very special feature of the present book, namely, in addition to all the wonderful words of the Bible we have the words and sayings of the Saints now in heaven who prayed and struggled as we do today, and if we dare say so, the Saints still living in the world today.

Each day's meditation and prayer are made up of a Scripture text, a saying from a Saint, and a prayer for some grace, together with illustrations as an inspirational touch.

This book then is presented to you in the hope of making Christ, the great ones in the Bible, and our fellow citizens—the Saints in heaven as well as those praying here on this earth—present to us in each day so that we may be one with them now and with God forever.

Rev. Frederick Schroeder

The wine ran out, and Jesus' mother . . . instructed those waiting on table, "Do whatever he tells you." —Jn 2:3-5

JAN.
1

REFLECTION. Let Mary never be far from your lips or your heart. And to obtain the fruit of her prayers, do not forget the example of her life.

With her support, you will never fall. Under her protection, you will never fear. Under her guidance, you will never tire. And with her help, you will reach your heavenly goal.

— *St. Bernard*

PRAYER. *Heavenly Father, keep me close to Your fairest daughter Mary all my life. Help me to reach Jesus through Mary.*

When the eighth day arrived for his circumcision, the name Jesus was given the child. —Lk 2:21

JAN.
2

REFLECTION. The name of Jesus is a name of joy. When the memory of our sins weighs us down, this name brings back our joy.

This mighty name reminds us that the Son of God became man to be our Savior.

— *St. Alphonsus Liguori*

PRAYER. *O Lord Jesus, may Your holy Name be ever in my thoughts, on my lips, and in my heart. Let it give me strength throughout life and especially at my death.*

JAN.
3

I came that they may have life and have it to the full. . . . Eternal life is this: to know you, the only true God, and him whom you have sent, Jesus Christ.

—Jn 10:10, 17:3

REFLECTION. The life that is proper to the Christian soul as well as the Christian family is the divine life. — *Pope Pius XII*

PRAYER. *Almighty God, help me to do always those works that lead to true life. Let me share in the life of the Trinity (Father, Son, and Holy Spirit) on earth and attain the fullness of that life forever in heaven.*

JAN.
4

When the Shepherd appears you will win for yourselves the unfading crown of glory. —1 Pt 5:4

REFLECTION. You are children of eternity. Your immortal crown awaits you, and the best of Fathers waits there to reward your duty and love.

You may indeed sow here in tears, but you may be sure there to reap in joy.

— *St. Elizabeth Ann Seton*

PRAYER. *Heavenly Father, thank You for making me a child of eternity. Help me to live each day in such a way that I may deserve to be a child of Yours forever.*

"Where is the newborn king of the Jews? We observed his star at its rising and have come to pay him tribute." —Mt 2:1-2

JAN. 5

REFLECTION. God's grace is a seed that we must not snuff out. We must cooperate with it.

This is especially true of those inspirations that lead us to make acts of virtue on some occasion. Such cooperation in grace is sometimes the very essence of our happiness.

— *Blessed Claude de la Colombiere*

PRAYER. *Heavenly Father, let me imitate the astrologers and be ever ready to cooperate with Your grace—whether it comes from outside or from my inner self.*

Entering the house, [they] found the child with Mary his mother. They prostrated themselves and did him homage. —Mt 2:9-11

JAN. 6

REFLECTION. If we approach with faith, we too will see Jesus . . .; for the Eucharistic table takes the place of the crib. Here the Body of the Lord is present, wrapped not in swaddling clothes but in the rays of the Holy Spirit.

— *St. John Chrysostom*

PRAYER. *Lord, God, teach me to see the living presence of Your Divine Son in the Eucharist. Make my faith so vivid that I will gladly come to encounter Jesus in every Mass.*

JAN. 7

If you want to avoid judgment, stop passing judgment. Your verdict on others will be the verdict passed on you. —Mt 7:1-2

REFLECTION. The rush to pass judgment should be avoided for two reasons.

It places the consciences of the judges in danger and also imperils the innocence of the accused.
— *St. Francis de Sales*

PRAYER. *O Lord, let me curb my desire to judge others. Help me to turn my judgments upon myself so that I may remain free from sin and receive a favorable judgment from You.*

JAN. 8

Your heavenly Father knows all that you need. Seek first his kingship over you, his way of holiness, and all these things will be given you besides. —Mt 6:33

REFLECTION. If we want to have true concern for our own spiritual and temporal interests, we must act as follows.

We must above all be concerned with the interests of God and look after our neighbor's good.
— *St. John Bosco*

PRAYER. *Dear Lord, let me not be closed up in my own self-interest. Help me to do always the things that are pleasing to You and good for others.*

Blessed are you when they insult you and persecute you ... because of me. Be glad and rejoice, for your reward is great in heaven.
—Mt 5:11-12

JAN. 9

REFLECTION. The heroes of the Gospel were persecuted because they proclaimed their faith in Jesus. They are the true wise men.

On earth they sowed their seed in humiliation and sorrow. One day they will reap with joy and rejoicing — *Bl. Theophane Venard*

PRAYER. *Lord Jesus, grant me the courage to confess my faith in Your name. Let me be always mindful of your presence.*

Enough, then, of worrying about tomorrow. Let tomorrow take care of itself. Today has troubles enough of its own. —Mt 6:34

JAN. 10

REFLECTION. Let us strive to make the present moment beautiful. —*St. Francis de Sales*

Let us especially regret the smallest amount of time that we waste or fail to use in loving God. — *St. John of the Cross*

PRAYER. *Lord God, help me to remember that yesterday is gone forever and tomorrow may never come. Let me live in the present and strive to do Your will.*

JAN. 11

What I tell you is this: do not swear at all. . . . Say, "Yes" when you mean "Yes" and "No" when you mean "No." Anything beyond that is from the evil one.

—Mt 5:34-37

REFLECTION. We must have such great love for the truth that our words will take on the character of oaths. — *St. Paulinus*

PRAYER. *Lord Jesus, You are the Truth. Grant me a great love for all truth. Let me devote my life to it and speak nothing but the truth at all times.*

JAN. 12

I solemnly assure you, unless the grain of wheat falls to the earth and dies, it remains just a grain of wheat. But if it dies, it produces much fruit. —Jn 12:24

REFLECTION. God has made human beings so noble that every suffering which purifies us and every effort which raises us up gladdens us while making us better. — *St. Augustine*

PRAYER. *Dear Jesus, help me to accept suffering after Your example, so that I may be made better by it. Let me unite myself to You in every suffering.*

Trust in the Lord with all your heart, on your own intelligence rely not. —Prv. 3:5

JAN. 13

REFLECTION. In our attempt to penetrate God's truth we are held within the bonds of ignorance by the weakness of our minds.

We comprehend Divine ideas by earnest attention to God's teaching and by obedience to the faith which carries us beyond mere human apprehension. — *St. Hilary*

PRAYER. *All-knowing God, grant me the grace to come to a better understanding of Your truths. Let me not only believe them but also carry them out daily in my life.*

Then will I go to the altar of God, the God of my gladness and youth. —Ps 43:4

JAN. 14

REFLECTION. We must strive to place ourselves completely in God's hands.

Then He will cause us to feel the effects of His goodness and protection—which are at times extraordinary.

– *St. John Baptist de la Salle.*

PRAYER. *Holy Lord, let me live constantly in Your presence. Grant that I may possess a spirit of joy and gladness because of the firm knowledge that You are always with me.*

JAN. 15

What father among you will give his son a snake if he asks for a fish?
—Lk 11:11

REFLECTION. It is not enough for Christian parents to nourish only the bodies of their children; even animals do this.

They must also nourish their souls in grace, in virtue, and in God's holy commandments.
— *St. Catherine of Siena.*

PRAYER. *Heavenly Father, give me some of Your infinite Fatherly concern for Your children. Teach me to inspire my children to know, love, and serve You.*

JAN. 16

O Lord, to you I call; hasten to me; hearken to my voice when I call upon you. Let my prayer come like incense before you
—Ps 141:1-2

REFLECTION. Prayer is the first expression of our inner truth, the first condition of authentic spiritual truth.

Prayer gives a meaning to the whole of life, at every moment, and in every circumstance.
— *Pope John Paul II*

PRAYER. *Almighty Father, let me realize that prayer is the breath of the divine life. Let me make use of it every day of my life.*

14

What can a man offer in exchange for his very life? —Mt 16:26

JAN. 17

REFLECTION.   Everything of this world is sold at its price or exchanged for another equivalently priced.

But the promise of life eternal is purchased at a bargain price!   *— St. Antony the Hermit*

PRAYER.   *Lord of all, help me to be willing to pay the price of receiving eternal life. Let me offer myself to You in all that I do and say each day.*

Just as the Father who has life sent me and I have life because of the Father, so the man who feeds on me will have life because of me. —Jn 6:57

JAN. 18

REFLECTION.   The Holy Eucharist is a fire that purifies and consumes all our miseries and imperfections.

Do Everything in your power to make yourself worthy of the Eucharist, and this Divine Fire will take care of the rest.

— St. Hyacinth of Mariscotti

PRAYER.   *Living God, You have given me the Eucharist as my food for heavenly life. Help me to partake of it often and so be strengthened on my pilgrim journey on earth.*

JAN.
19

Why have you been standing here idle all day? —Mt 20:6

REFLECTION. Water that does not flow and comes to a halt in holes becomes stagnant and filled with impurities.

In the same way, the body that is worn down by prolonged idleness produces and fuels the fire of covetousness and illicit pleasure.
— *St. Bernard*

PRAYER. *Ever-creating Father, help me to work diligently every day of my life. Grant that I may always shun idleness as the devil's workshop, and do my bit to build up the world in accord with Your holy Will.*

JAN.
20

The Father already loves you, because you have loved me and have believed that I came from God. —Jn 16:27

REFLECTION. Thinking about God is not really hard, for we normally think about those we love.

I like to meditate on the *Our Father*. It is so good to dwell on the fact that God is our Father. — *St. Theresa of the Child Jesus*

PRAYER. *Heavenly Lord, help me to realize that You are really a Father to all human beings. Let me never doubt Your overflowing love for me and try to return that love to You.*

16

Faith is confident assurance concerning what we hope for, and conviction about things we do not see. —Heb 11:1

JAN. 21

REFLECTION. Unless we possess the light of faith, we will walk in darkness.

We will be like the blind for whom the day has become night. — *St. Catherine of Siena.*

PRAYER. *Faithful God, grant me the light of Your faith. Let me believe in You who cannot deceive or be deceived, and ever enjoy the fruits of true faith.*

Had not your law been my delight, I should have perished in my affliction. —Ps 119:92

JAN. 22

REFLECTION. Meditation renders life honest and well-ordered and imparts knowledge of human and divine things. — *St. Bernard*

PRAYER. *Loving Father, help me to meditate on divine things every day. Grant that I may set aside special moments when I am conscious only of Your sacred presence and myself.*

17

JAN 23

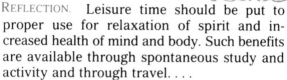

There is an appointed time for everything, . . . a time to weep, and a time to laugh, a time to mourn, and a time to dance.

—Eccl 3:1, 4

REFLECTION. Leisure time should be put to proper use for relaxation of spirit and increased health of mind and body. Such benefits are available through spontaneous study and activity and through travel. . . .

These benefits are also obtained from physical exercise and sports events.

— *Vatican II: Church in the Modern World, 61*

PRAYER. *Timeless Lord, teach me to value every moment that You graciously allot to me in this life. Let me never waste or misuse the least part of it.*

JAN. 24

Take my yoke upon your shoulders and learn from me, for I am gentle and humble of heart.

—Mt 11:29-30

REFLECTION. If there was something better than meekness, God would certainly have told us.

But He exhorts us above all to be meek and humble of heart. — *St. Francis de Sales*

PRAYER. *Lord Jesus, teach me what true meekness entails. Inspire me to practice it after your example in all circumstances of my life.*

While we have the opportunity, let us do good to all men—especially those of the household of the faith. —Gal 6:10

JAN. 25

REFLECTION. Courtesy is one of the properties of God, Who sends His sun and rain to the just and the unjust through courtesy.

Courtesy is the sister of charity, by which hatred is overcome and love is prized.

— *St. Francis of Assisi*

PRAYER. *God of kindness, help me to make Christian courtesy the rule of my life. Let me show that courtesy to all in every circumstance—so that I may truly imitate You.*

You are the light of the world. . . . Your light must shine before men so that they may see goodness in your acts and give praise to your heavenly Father. —Mt 5:14, 16

JAN. 26

REFLECTION. It would scarcely be necessary to teach doctrine if our lives were radiant enough.

If we behaved like true Christians, there would be no pagans. — *Pope John XXIII*

PRAYER. *Father of lights, let my life be illumined by the light of Christ. And enable me to radiate that life to others in all my works.*

JAN. 27

The servant of the Lord must not be quarrelsome but must be kindly toward all. —2 Tm 2:24

REFLECTION. Exercise pleasantness toward all, taking great care especially that what you have commanded may never be done by reason of force.

For God has given free will to everyone, and therefore never forces anyone—but only indicates, calls, and persuades. — *St. Angela Merici.*

PRAYER. *Heavenly Father, teach me how to deal pleasantly with those I command. Help me to persuade rather than attempt to force others to do what must be done.*

———

JAN. 28

Obedience is better than sacrifice, and submission than the fat of rams. —1 Sm 15:22

REFLECTION. Obedience unites us so closely to God that it in a way transforms us into Him, so that we have no other will but His.

If obedience is lacking, even prayer cannot be pleasing to God. — *St. Thomas Aquinas*

PRAYER. *Omniscient Lord, teach me to value obedience to Your laws and Your will. Grant that I may be completely obedient to You in all things.*

You need patience to do God's will and receive what he has promised. —Heb 10:36

JAN. 29

REFLECTION. Patience is the marrow or core of charity.

There is no charity without patience. Neither is there patience without charity.

— St. Catherine of Siena

PRAYER. *God of infinite patience, help me to do Your will in patience. Teach me to be patient with others out of love for You.*

Let them grow together until harvest; then . . . I will order the harvesters, first collect the weeds and bundle them up to burn, then gather the wheat into my barn. —Mt 13:30

JAN. 30

REFLECTION. While there is still time, correct your faults and endure patiently what you cannot correct completely.

Give yourself to prayer while waiting for the Lord Himself to provide—either by correcting now or by correcting at the end-time harvest.

— St. Augustine

PRAYER. *Just Father, teach me how to administer correction according to Your will. Let me proceed with prudence and prayer in removing any evil I may encounter among others.*

21

JAN. 31

Whoever welcomes one such child for my sake welcomes me.
—Mt 18:5-6

REFLECTION. Do you want to do something good and holy—indeed very holy and divine?

Then work for the salvation of all young people. — *St. John Bosco*

PRAYER. *Heavenly Father, help me to see You in all children as well as in all human beings. And let me work to bring forth Your image and likeness in them.*

FEB. 1

Whatever you ask the Father, he will give you in my name. . . . Ask and you shall receive.
—Jn 16:23-24

REFLECTION. Prayer is a great good. For when we speak to a person endowed with virtue, we receive much benefit.

How much greater benefits will flow on persons who speak with God. For prayer is speaking with God. — *St. John Chrysostom*

PRAYER. *Heavenly Father, help me to pray to you through Jesus and in the Holy Spirit. Let me be faithful to my daily conversation with You.*

I find my joy in the suffering I endure for you. In my own flesh I fill up what is lacking in the sufferings of Christ for the sake of his body, the church. —Col 1:24

FEB.

2

REFLECTION. Christ made me understand that I could save souls through the cross.

The greater the crosses I encountered, the more ardent became my desire to endure them. — *St. Theresa of the Child Jesus*

PRAYER. *Lord, in Your wisdom, You have given us the opportunity to suffer with Jesus. Help me to offer my sufferings for the salvation of souls.*

Be on your guard against false prophets, who come to you in sheeps' clothing but underneath are wolves on the prowl. You will know them by their deeds.

—Mt 7:15-16

FEB.

3

REFLECTION The Apostle Paul tells us that the fruits of the works of the flesh are: fornication, uncleanness, lust, idolatry, and enmity.

The fruits that will identify the good tree are: charity, joy, peace, benignity, faith, meekness, and continency. — *St. Augustine*

PRAYER. *Almighty God, let me labor always to bring forth good fruits and ever shun the evil fruits of the works of the flesh.*

23

FEB. 4

Has anyone hoped in the Lord and been disappointed? —Sir 2:10

REFLECTION. Those who trust in Jesus are as simple as children. They cling to His garments and in every difficulty have recourse to him.

Filled with trust, they exclaim: "Help me, Lord Jesus, to overcome this enemy and this obstacle. You alone can help me and I am sure that You want to do so." — *St. Francis de Sales*

PRAYER. *Lord Jesus, let me put all my hopes in You. By Your Cross and Resurrection You have given hope to the world.*

FEB. 5

In the way of your decrees I rejoice, as much as in all riches. —Ps 119:14

REFLECTION. It is certainly true that the Christian Religion given us from heaven with its laws is intended to lead us to eternal happiness.

However, it is also incontestable that this Religion fills our present life with untold benefits. — *Pope Pius XII*

PRAYER. *O God, You are the Supreme Legislator of the world. Help me to keep Your laws which insure my earthly and my heavenly happiness.*

You love justice and hate wickedness; therefore God, your God, has anointed you with the oil of gladness. —Ps 45:8

FEB.
6

REFLECTION. The rule of justice is plain: a good person ought never to swerve from the truth.

Neither ought the just person inflict any unjust loss on anyone, nor act in any deceitful and fraudulent way. — *St. Ambrose*

PRAYER. *Lord of Justice, grant that I may render to all people what is due them. Let me thus have a share in Your infinite Justice.*

Were not all ten [lepers] made whole? Where are the other nine? Was there no one to return and give thanks to God except this foreigner? —Lk 17:17-18

FEB.
7

REFLECTION. Ingratitude to God is the enemy of the soul.

It divests the soul of merits, dissipates its virtues, and deprives it of graces. — *St. Bernard*

PRAYER. *God of all goodness, let me always take care to give proper thanks to You. Grant that I may do so through the Eucharist and through my own private prayers every day.*

FEB.
8

If you had faith . . . , you would be able to say to this mountain, 'Move from here to there,' and it would move. Nothing would be impossible for you. —Mt 17:20

REFLECTION. God does not work in those who refuse to place all their confidence and hope in him alone.

But He imparts the fullness of His love upon those who possess a deep faith and hope. For them He does great things. — *St. Jerome Emiliani*

PRAYER. *God of power and might, let me place all my trust in You. Strengthen my faith and deepen my hope that You may be able to bring about the wonderful things You want to do for me.*

FEB.
9

By patient endurance you will save your lives. —Lk 21:19

REFLECTION. Practice patience toward everyone, and especially toward yourself.

Never be disturbed because of your imperfections, but always get up bravely after a fall.
— *St. Francis de Sales*

PRAYER. *God of Patience, let me endure my imperfections without rebelling. Help me to be patient with myself as well as with others.*

How blest are the poor in spirit: the reign of God is theirs.

—Mt 5:3

FEB. 10

REFLECTION. Some persons, because of their state of life, cannot be without wealth and position.

They must at least keep their heart free of love for such things — *St. Angela*

PRAYER. *Loving Father, help me to use the things of this world without being overly attached to them. Teach me to set my heart on heavenly things.*

If God clothes in such splendor the grass of the field . . . , how much more will he provide for you!

—Lk 12:28

FEB. 11

REFLECTION. Providence is the care God takes of all existing things. —*St. John Damascene*

Entrust the past to God's mercy, the present to His love, and the future to His Providence. — *St. Augustine*

PRAYER. *All-provident God, I entrust my whole life into Your loving care. Calm all my anxieties and keep me safe in You.*

27

FEB. 12

Search the Scriptures in which you think you have eternal life—they also testify on my behalf.

—Jn 5:39

REFLECTION. Reading the Scriptures is a wonderful thing.

The mind of the Scriptures can never be exhausted. It is a well without a bottom.

— *St. John Chrysostom*

PRAYER. *Lord Jesus, You are the Word of God. When I read the Scriptures, let me see You on every page and learn to become ever more like You.*

FEB. 13

I was ill and you comforted me. . . . As often as you did it for one of my least brothers, you did it for me.

—Mt 25:36, 40

REFLECTION. Before all things and above all things care must be taken of the sick.

They must be served in every deed as Christ Himself.

— *St. Benedict*

PRAYER. *Jesus, infinite Healer, teach me to visit and comfort the sick. Help me always to see You in them and not count the cost.*

On that day you will know that I am in my Father, and you are in me, and I in you. —Jn 14:20

**FEB.
14**

REFLECTION. Jesus Christ must live in us, and we must live only in Him.

His life must be our life, and our life must be a continuation and expression of His life.

— St. John Eudes

PRAYER. *Lord Jesus, make me realize that You are living in me and I am in You. Enable me to radiate You in my outward life by being consciously united to You in my inner life.*

The grace of God . . . trains us to reject godless ways and worldly desires, and live temperately, justly, and devoutly. —Ti 3:11-12

**FEB.
15**

REFLECTION. The spirit of Jesus Christ is a spirit of righteousness and sincerity.

All who are called to glorify this saving God must act in accord with that spirit.

— St. Vincent de Paul

PRAYER. *Lord Jesus, grant me the grace to act in accord with Your spirit of righteousness and sincerity. Enable me to reject godless ways and worldly desires in every form.*

FEB. 16

Those who belong to Christ Jesus have crucified their flesh with its passions and desires. —Gal 5:24

REFLECTION. The definition of vice is as follows:

It is the wrong use—in violation of the Lord's command—of what has been given us by God for a good purpose. — *St. Basil*

PRAYER. *All-holy God, help me to curb my passions and desires. Let me always use your gifts in the way You intended for them to be used.*

FEB. 17

Although the Israelites had given [the Gibeonites] their oath, Saul had attempted to kill them off in his zeal. —2 Sm 21:2

REFLECTION. Zeal without knowledge is always less useful and effective than regulated zeal.

Indeed, very often such zeal is highly dangerous. — *St. Bernard*

PRAYER. *Most zealous Father, instill me with holy zeal based upon true knowledge. Let me never act out of intemperate and impetuous zeal.*

If you love those who love you, what credit is that to you? Even sinners love those who love them.

FEB.
18

—Lk 6:32

REFLECTION. A love that overflows from abundance and generosity is more acceptable than one aroused by the aridity of need.

The latter derives from misery; the former from mercy. — *St. Augustine*

PRAYER. *God of love, help me to imitate Your merciful love for us. Let me strive to manifest a selfless love toward other humans because they are Your creatures.*

I am the vine, you are the branches. He who lives in me, and I in him, will produce abundantly.

FEB.
19

— Jn 15:5

REFLECTION. Through the Eucharist, Jesus rules over all his faithful.

His truth is the light of their minds. His divine law is the invariable and inflexible law of their wills. His love is the noble passion of their hearts. — *St. Peter Eymard*

PRAYER. *Eucharistic Lord, come into my heart and rule over my whole life. Grant that I may live in You and You may live in me forever.*

FEB. 20

When you fast, . . . groom your hair and wash your face. . . . Your father, who sees what is hidden will repay you. —Mt 6:17-18

REFLECTION. Fasting [when rightly practiced] lifts the mind to God and mortifies the flesh.

It makes virtue easy to attain and increases our merits. — *St. Francis de Sales*

PRAYER. *Heavenly Father, help me to fast for the right reason. Teach me to fast to curb illicit desires and to obtain closer union with You.*

FEB. 21

For whom the Lord loves he reproves, he chastises the son he favors. —Prv 3:12

REFLECTION. When you are scorned by others and lashed by God, do not despair.

God lashes us in this life to shield us from the eternal lash in the next. — *St. Peter Damian*

PRAYER. *Infinitely just God, help me to accept Your corrections and turn them to my benefit. Let me never despair about my weaknesses, but entrust myself to Your goodness and mercy.*

Almsgiving frees one from death, and keeps one from going into the dark abode. —Tb 4:10

FEB.
22

REFLECTION. If we want to take genuine care of our spiritual and temporal interests, we act as follows.

We should always pursue God's interests and through almsgiving procure the temporal good of our neighbor. — *St. John Bosco*

PRAYER. *Beneficent Father, help me to share with others the goods in my possession. Let me freely give out of love for You what I have freely received from You.*

There is a time and a judgment for everything. —Eccl 8:6

FEB.
23

REFLECTION. Help one another with the generosity of the Lord, and despise no one.

When you have an opportunity to do good, do not let it go by. — *St. Polycarp*

PRAYER. *God of goodness, let me never allow an opportunity for good to be wasted. Help me take advantage of every moment at my disposal to do good.*

FEB. 24

God sent forth his Son born of a woman, born under the law, to deliver from the law those who were subjected to it. —Gal 4:4-5

REFLECTION. God has decreed that the whole of Redemption should be accomplished through Mary, with Mary, and in Mary.

Just as nothing was created without Christ, so nothing has been re-created without the Virgin. — *St. John of the Cross*

PRAYER. *Heavenly Father, help me never to cease having recourse to the Blessed Virgin Mary. Let me keep ever in mind that she is Your beloved daughter, Spouse of the Holy Spirit, and Mother of Your Son.*

FEB. 25

In truth and love, then, we shall have grace, mercy, and peace from God the Father and from Jesus Christ, the Father's Son.
—2 Jn 1

REFLECTION. Our thoughts must be centered on the search for truth and our affections on the fervor of love.

In this way, we will always be practicing divine love. — *St. Bernard*

PRAYER. *All-loving Father, let me ever be open to Your truth and Your love. Enable me to walk all my days in that love and that truth.*

A faithful friend is a life-saving remedy, . . . for he who fears God behaves accordingly, and his friend will be like himself.

FEB. 26

—Sir 6:16-17

REFLECTION. It is an effect of God's Providence that human beings cannot do without one another.

This necessity for mutual assistance unites them more closely to one another by ties of friendship. — *St. John Chrysostom*

PRAYER. *God of goodness, help me to remember that my greatest Friend is Jesus. Let my relation to Him underlie my relations with all my friends and keep us faithful to one another.*

You have drawn near . . . to the heavenly Jerusalem . . . to Jesus, the mediator of a new covenant.

FEB. 27

—Heb 12:23-24

REFLECTION. Let us rise above the things that pass away. Up above, the air is so pure.

Jesus can hide Himself but we will find Him there. — *St. Theresa of the Child Jesus*

PRAYER. *Heavenly Father, amid the dizzying events and circumstances of daily life, let me keep my eyes on Jesus. Help me to rely on Him always, for He is my Redeemer.*

FEB. 28

Whoever wishes to be my follower must . . . take up his cross each day and follow in my footsteps. —Lk 9:23

REFLECTION. Let the primary desire of your heart be to stir up in yourselves an ardent and affectionate desire to imitate Jesus in all your works.

Strive to do everything as the Lord Himself would do. — *St. John of the Cross.*

PRAYER. *Lord, Jesus, help me to pattern my life after You. Grant that I may imitate You completely—in all my thoughts, words, and deeds.*

MAR. 1

He who is not with me is against me, and he who does not gather with me scatters. —Lk 11:23

REFLECTION. The devil desires to keep souls prisoners but the Lord desires to set them free. The devil incites us to evil but the Savior invites us to practice good

What accord is there between works that are so contrary! — *St Jerome*

PRAYER. *My Lord and my Savior, let me never give up the freedom from sin which You won for me. Help me to cling to You and shun all contact with evil.*

Honesty opens my lips. Yes, the truth my mouth recounts.

MAR. 2

—Prv 8:6

REFLECTION. Our love for truth must be very great.

So great in fact that all our words must possess the value of oaths. — *St. Paulinus*

PRAYER. *Father of all truth, teach me to revere the truth, in my life. Let me avoid falsehood in any form.*

Conduct yourselves . . . in a way worthy of the gospel of Christ, . . . exerting yourselves with one accord for the faith of the gospel.

MAR. 3

—Phil 1:27

REFLECTION. The more the Gospel is read, the more faith becomes alive.

The Gospel is the book which serves all and for all. — *St. Pius X*

PRAYER. *Lord Jesus, grant me Your grace to believe in the Gospel and to read that Gospel continually. Then let me put it into practice in my life.*

MAR. 4

I consider the sufferings of the present to be as nothing compared with the glory to be revealed in us.
—Rom 8:18

REFLECTION. The desire to receive God's treasures and favors is universal.

But how few people aspire to wear themselves out and to suffer for the Son of God!

— *St. John of the Cross*

PRAYER. *Loving Father, help me to spend myself out of love for You and Your Son. Enable me to endure sufferings patiently in imitation of Him and in anticipation of the glory to come.*

MAR. 5

The Lord is far from the wicked, but the prayer of the just he hears.
—Prv 15:29

REFLECTION. Let us unceasingly prepare ourselves for prayer by carrying out our duties with great fidelity.

Then let us come before our divine Savior with all the simplicity of our souls.

— *St. Mary Euphrase*

PRAYER. *Almighty God, move me to prepare myself for prayer by a good life. Grant that I may pray to You by my works as well as my words.*

I am the sheepgate. . . . Whoever enters [the sheepfold] through me will be safe. —Jn 10:7, 9

MAR. 6

REFLECTION. We must take refuge in the adorable Heart of our Good Shepherd.

Let us go to Him like little sheep who seek the safety of their sheepfold against the infernal world. — *St. Margaret Mary Alacoque*

PRAYER. *Lord Jesus, call me into Your sheepfold and take care of me. Keep me safe amid the troubles of life and secure from the evil one.*

Let my heart rejoice in your salvation; let me sing of the Lord, "He has been good to me." —Ps 13:6

MAR. 7

REFLECTION. The blood of the humble and immaculate Lamb takes away any doubt we might have about God wanting solely our good.

And how could the Supreme God do anything other than good? — *St. Catherine of Siena*

PRAYER. *Father of all goodness, grant that I may appreciate Your great goodness toward me both in the natural and in the supernatural sphere. Let me learn to praise You continually.*

MAR. 8

If you are unfaithful, [Christ] will still remain faithful. —2 Tm 2:13

REFLECTION. Whether you like it or not, you will grow apart from human beings.

However, Christ is faithful and always with you. For Christ provides all things.

— *St. John of God*

PRAYER. *Lord Jesus, help me to remain faithful to You rather than to trust in others. However, should I ever be unfaithful, please continue to be faithful to Your promises and grant me the grace to do penance.*

MAR. 9

Teach me to do your will, for you are my God. —Ps 143:10

REFLECTION. Let us serve God, but let us do so according to His will.

He will then take the place of everything in our lives. He will be our strength, and the reward of our labors. — *St. Vincent de Paul.*

PRAYER. *Infinite Lord, help me to serve You always in accord with Your holy will. Show me how to make You my Lord and my All.*

We are . . . heirs of God, heirs of Christ, if only we suffer with him so as to be glorified with him.

MAR. 10

—Rom 8:17

REFLECTION.   If we suffer with Christ, we will be glorified with Him.

The fulfillment of the promised happiness is certain for those who share in the Lord's Passion.
— *St. Leo the Great*

PRAYER.   *Grant me Your grace to overcome my natural fear of suffering. Strengthen me to bear my sufferings in union with Your sacred Passion for the salvation of the world.*

Why look at the speck in your brother's eye when you miss the plank in your own?

MAR. 11

—Mt 7:3

REFLECTION.   Never suspect your brothers or sisters of any evil.

For suspicion poisons the purity of one's heart.
— *St. Thomas Aquinas*

PRAYER.   *God of goodness, help me to avoid being suspicious of others. Teach me to accept all persons for what they are—Your children, potential members of Christ, and temples of the Holy Spirit.*

MAR. 12

For his sake I have forfeited everything, . . . so that Christ may be my wealth and I may be in him.

—Phil 3;8-9

REFLECTION. An act of renunciation is an act of union with God.

The Divine Master looks lovingly upon a person who gains a victory over self.

— *St. Madeleine Sophie Barat*

PRAYER. *Divine Master, teach me to give up all things so that I may be united closely to You. Let me be willing to lose all things rather than give up my union with You.*

MAR. 13

God can multiply his favors among you so that you may always have enough of everything and even a surplus for good works.

—2 Cor 9:8

REFLECTION. God rewards all our good works in His own way.

This way invariably provides us with an opportunity to accomplish even better works.

— *St. Theresa of Avila*

PRAYER. *All-provident Lord, help me never to squander Your grace. Let me continually accomplish the good works that You both envision for me and assist me to do.*

Now is the acceptable time! Now is the time of salvation! **MAR. 14**

—2 Cor 6:2

REFLECTION. You no longer have the time that is past. Nor are you sure of the time that is to come.

Hence, all you do have is this present point in time and nothing more.

— *St. Catherine of Siena*

PRAYER. *Timeless Lord, teach me to be grateful for every moment of time that You allot to me. Grant that I may always make the best use of my time.*

All Scripture is inspired of God and is useful for teaching—for reproof, correction, and training in holiness. **MAR. 15**

—2 Tm 3:16

REFLECTION. All Christians must refer always and everywhere to Scripture for all their choices, becoming like children before it.

They should seek in it the most effective remedy against all their weaknesses and not dare take a step without being illumined by the divine rays of those words. — *Pope John Paul II*

PRAYER. *God of wisdom, move me to have recourse constantly to Your words in Scripture. Let me find light, strength, and consolation in this sacred Book that was inspired by You.*

43

MAR. 16

His eyes are upon the ways of man, and he beholds all his steps.

—Jb 34:21

REFLECTION. Your eyes, O Lord, have a true view of people.

This is what they really are—and nothing more. — *St. Francis de Sales*

PRAYER. *All-knowing Lord, let me realize that my real self is only what I am in Your eyes. Give me a true picture of that self and inspire me to become better day by day.*

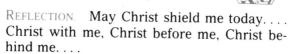

MAR. 17

As long as you neglected to do it to one of these least ones, you neglected to do it to me.

—Mt 25:45

REFLECTION. May Christ shield me today.... Christ with me, Christ before me, Christ behind me....

Christ in the mouth of everyone who speaks of me, Christ in every eye that sees me, Christ in every ear that hears me. — *St. Patrick*

PRAYER. *Lord Jesus, be with me this day and let me see You in everyone I meet. Grant that I may always serve You in others and so arrive at Your heavenly Kingdom where I will serve You personally forever.*

You are a gracious and merciful **MAR**
God, slow to anger, rich in clemency, and loathe to punish.
—Jon 4:2

18

REFLECTION. The Lord is loving toward human beings; He is quick to pardon but slow to punish.

Therefore, no persons should ever despair of their own salvation. — *St. Cyril of Jerusalem*

PRAYER. *Merciful Lord, come to my aid quickly in time of despair. Let me rely on the infinite merits of Your Son, Who died for me.*

Joseph her husband [was] an up- **MAR.**
right man.
—Mt 1:19

19

REFLECTION. Saint Joseph was the just man by his constant fidelity, an effect of justice; by his perfect discretion, a sister to prudence; by his upright conduct, a mark of strength; and by his inviolable chastity, a flower of temperance. — *St. Albert the Great*

PRAYER. *Lord of Justice, enable me to be a just and upright person after the example of St. Joseph. Let me be just toward You, toward myself, and toward all human beings.*

MAR.
20

In the beginning . . . *God created*
the heavens and the earth.

—Gn 1:1

REFLECTION. The enigmas contained in the physical universe postulate and indicate the existence of an infinitely superior Spirit.

This divine Spirit creates, conserves, governs, and consequently knows and scrutinizes in a supreme intuition—today as at the dawn of the first day of creation—all that exists.

— *Pope Pius XII*

PRAYER. *Almighty God, You created the whole world to show Your power and overflowing love. Enable me to see You in every part of creation and to sing praise to You constantly.*

MAR.
21

What profit does a man show
who gains the whole world and
destroys himself in the process?

—Mk 8:34

REFLECTION. True riches do not consist in worldly wealth.

They consist in the virtues that we make part of our lives and that will become our eternal treasure.

— *St. Bernard*

PRAYER. *All-holy God, teach me the value of true riches. Let me labor not to store up worldly wealth but to amass Christian virtues that will make me truly rich for all eternity.*

Rejoice . . . in the measure that you share Christ's sufferings. When his glory is revealed, you will rejoice exultantly. —1 Pt 4:13

MAR. 22

REFLECTION. Let us strive to face suffering with Christian courage.

Then all difficulties will vanish and pain itself will become transformed into joy.

— *St. Theresa of Avila*

PRAYER. *Jesus, Man of Sorrows, in every suffering keep my eyes fixed on You. Let me keep ever before my mind the glory to come and so face the suffering with true Christian courage.*

Athletes deny themselves all sorts of things. . . . What I do is discipline my body and master it.

—1 Cor 9:25-26

MAR. 23

REFLECTION. All Christians are called to mortify our natural inclinations.

If we do so, we draw down upon ourselves supernatural inspirations. — *St. Francis de Sales*

PRAYER. *Merciful Father, help me to keep a tight reign over my evil inclinations. Grant that I may thus receive Your graces and live in accord with Your will.*

MAR.
24

My eyes are ever toward the Lord for he will free my feet from the snare.
                                        —Ps 25:15

REFLECTION.   Let us never forget that the measure of our recollection will be the measure of our virtue.

Indeed, it will be the measure of God's life in us.   — *St. Peter Eymard*

PRAYER.   *Loving Father, teach me how to be truly recollected in You. Inspire me to keep my heart and mind on You constantly as I go about my daily tasks.*

MAR.
25

I am the servant of the Lord. Let it be done to me as you say.
                                        —Lk 1:38

REFLECTION.   We should harbor a single "Yes" concerning all that God wills and a single "No" concerning all that He does not will.

The state of things comprises perpetual communion   — *St. Vincent de Paul*

PRAYER.   *Lord Jesus, You became man when Mary gave her consent to the angel's announcement. Help me to give a perpetual consent to all that You will for me and a perpetual refusal to all that You do not will for me.*

Come, all you who pass by the way, look and see whether there is any suffering like my suffering.

MAR. 26

—Lam 1:12

REFLECTION. Human beings will never comprehend sufficiently the anguish and immensity of Mary's sorrows.

Very few Christians partake of those sufferings and even fewer offer any consolation to her.
— *St. Bridget*

PRAYER. *Lord Jesus, let me dwell constantly on Mary's part in the Redemption which entailed great sorrow for her. Teach me to imitate her in this respect and compassionate with her in her sufferings.*

Seek counsel from every wise man, and do not think lightly of any advice that can be useful.

MAR. 27

—Tb 4:18

REFLECTION. When we rashly decide to follow only our own lights, our reason deceives us and even the wisest persons go astray.

We should therefore seek the spiritual direction of others.
— *St. Bernard.*

PRAYER. *Lord of wisdom, let me never rely on my own conceits. Grant that I may seek spiritual direction from Your priests and others whom You have given us for this purpose.*

MAR.
28

*May I never boast of anything but
the cross of our Lord Jesus Christ.*

—Gal 6:14

REFLECTION. Devout souls cling wholeheartedly to the cross with Christ.

They thus acquire the most abundant fruits
of the Redemption for themselves and for
others. — *Pope Pius XI*

PRAYER. *Lord Jesus, You endured crucifixion
for the salvation of the world. Grant that I may
love and share Your Cross on earth so that I
may join You in glory in heaven.*

MAR.
29

*Let him who would boast, boast
in the Lord.* —1 Cor. 1:31

REFLECTION. Let us not take inordinate pride
in our successes.

If good flour issues from my mill, I must give
all the glory to the Lord. It is his hand that
pours the water that makes the grindstone
turn and sets every machine in motion.

— *St. Francies Xavier*

PRAYER. *Lord of the universe, make me ever
aware that Your inspirations cover the world
and account for all human success. Let me
give You thanks for any achievements I may
attain.*

Cast me not off in my old age; as my strength fails, forsake me not.
—Ps 71:9

MAR. 30

REFLECTION. When people age, everything gradually leaves them, but God comes to them.

Eternity also comes—with its duration without end and its day without night.

— *St. Francis de Sales*

PRAYER. *Ageless Lord, let me not fear old age with its many diminishments. Enable me to embrace it as the last state before my entrance into a new and endless life.*

Hope in God! for I shall again be thanking him in the presence of my savior and my God. —Ps 42:6

MAR. 31

REFLECTION. Go to the holy Table with your poverty and all your troubles—but also with hope and love.

These are the best dispositions that you can bring to the Eucharist. — *St. Peter Eymard*

PRAYER. *Heavenly Father, in evey Eucharist let me offer myself to You with all my joys and sorrows and in union with Jesus. Grant that with every Eucharist I participate in I may know, love, and live the Mass more.*

APR.
1

The man who loves his life loses it, while the man who hates his life in this world preserves it to life eternal.
—Jn 12:25

REFLECTION. There are Christians who are still puffed up with inordinate self-love.

Such persons should not think that they have achieved renunciation of self or that they are really following Jesus Christ.

— *St. John of the Cross*

PRAYER. *Heavenly Father, uproot in me all inordinate love of self. Enable me to have a true Christian attitude toward myself, so that I may really be a follower of Your Son.*

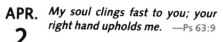

APR.
2

My soul clings fast to you; your right hand upholds me. —Ps 63:9

REFLECTION. Love of God inflames us with a desire to contemplate His beauty.

This contemplation is in turn the cause of greater love for God on our part.

— *St. Thomas Aquinas*

PRAYER. *God of goodness, teach me to love You with all my heart, mind, and soul. Grant that I may ardently desire to contemplate You and grow in Your love.*

Whatever you do, whether in speech or in action, do it in the name of the Lord Jesus. —Col 3:17

APR. 3

REFLECTION.   Some people say: "I wish I didn't have to be occupied with temporal things."

Yet the truth is that things are only temporal when we make them temporal.

— *St. Catherine of Siena*

PRAYER.   *Lord of the universe, teach me to convert all things into instruments of Your grace. Let me do everything for Christ and thus change temporal things into religious things.*

Have just men for your . . . companions; in the fear of God be your glory. —Sir 9:16

APR. 4

REFLECTION.   Seek the association of persons who are good.

For if you are the companion of their life, you will also be the companion of their virtue.

— *St. Isidore*

PRAYER.   *God of goodness, help me to be continually in the company of true Christians. Let me be edified by their virtues and their works, and let our association bring us all to heavenly glory.*

**APR.
5**

Love the Lord your God with all your heart. . . . Love your neighbor as yourself. —Mk 12:30-31

REFLECTION. If you truly want to help the soul of your neighbor, approach God first with all your heart.

Ask him simply to fill you with love, the greatest of all virtues; with it you can accomplish what you desire. — *St. Vincent Ferrer*

PRAYER. *Heavenly Father, grant me the grace to love You above all things and to do all my actions out of love for You. Help me to love others and work for their salvation.*

**APR.
6**

Through baptism into [Christ's] death we were buried with him, so that, just as Christ was raised from the dead . . . we too might live a new life. —Rom 6:4

REFLECTION. Christ is our life. Let us therefore look to Christ.

He came to suffer in order to merit glory; to seek contempt in order to be exalted. He came to die but also to rise again. — *St. Augustine*

PRAYER. *Heavenly Father, through my baptism I was buried with Christ and rose to a new life of grace. Let me so guard that life that I will enjoy it fully in heaven with Christ.*

Jesus offered one sacrifice for sins and took his seat forever at the right hand of God. —Heb 10:12

APR.

7

REFLECTION. When you are at Mass, be there as if you were on Calvary.

For it is the same sacrifice and the same Jesus Christ Who is doing for you what He did on the Cross for all human beings.

— *St. John Baptist de la Salle*

PRAYER. *Jesus, my Redeemer, at each Mass let me thank You for the supreme sacrifice You offered to free me from sin. Help me to be sorry for my sins and to resolve to follow You more closely.*

By his "will," we have been sanctified through the offering of the body of Jesus Christ.

—Heb 10:10

APR.

8

REFLECTION. God's infinite power, his profound wisdom, and the reign of his justice were known.

However, the dimensions of his clemency were not yet known. Jesus came as interpreter of the Divinity. — *St. Bernard*

PRAYER. *Merciful Father, let me not spurn Your clemency which You sent us in Jesus Christ. Grant that Christ's loving sacrifice may bear fruit in me in accord with Your will for me.*

APR.

9

He touched their eyes and said, "Because of your faith it shall be done to you," and they received their sight. —Mt 9:29-30

REFLECTION. The blind men cried out to Christ and overcame the cries of the crowd.

Such is the nature of faith that the greater are the obstacles it encounters, the more ardent it becomes. — *St. Charles Borromeo*

PRAYER. *Heavenly Father, grant me a living faith in the Good News of Jesus. Let it overcome all obstacles and become deeper every day of my life.*

APR.

10

God said: "Let there be light," and there was light. God saw how good the light was. —Gn 1:3-4

REFLECTION. Blest may You be, O Lord, with all Your creatures, especially my lord and brother Sun, who makes the day and by whom You give us light.

He is beautiful, radiant with great splendor: and he is the symbol of You, Most High.

— *St. Francis of Assisi*

PRAYER. *O God of infinite brightness, let me give You thanks for Your magnificent gift of light and of all creation. Help me always to use it wisely and well*

I know my sheep and my sheep know me . . . ; for these sheep I will give my life. —Jn 10:14-15

APR.
11

REFLECTION. Jesus, the Good Shepherd, is at the same time light and love.

That is to say, He is the truth in charity.

— *Pope Pius XII*

PRAYER. *Lord Jesus, let me be attached to You in truth and love. Grant that I may always follow You as my Shepherd amid the perils and trials of this life.*

A faithful friend is a sturdy shelter; he who finds one finds a treasure. —Sir 6:14

APR.
12

REFLECTION. Nothing on earth can stamp out true friendship.

Time itself cannot destroy such friendship, but instead finds it always and everywhere indomitable. — *St. Bernard*

PRAYER. *God of goodness, send me a true friend—one who has You as a friend too. And let me be a true friend on my part—so that our friendship will be indomitable.*

APR. 13

He told them, "This kind [of evil] you can drive out only by prayer."
—Mk 9:29

REFLECTION. This conclusion is obvious to all Christians:

A virtuous life is simply impossible without the aid of prayer. — *St. John Chrysostom*

PRAYER. *Almighty God, let me be convinced of the need for prayer in my life. Help me to turn to You often in prayer and lead a virtuous life.*

APR. 14

We know that God makes all things work together for the good of those who love him. —Rom 8:28

REFLECTION. Do not allow yourselves to be overly saddened by the unfortunate accidents of this world.

You are not aware of the benefits that they bring and by what secret judgment of God they are arranged for the eternal joy of the Elect. — *St. John of the Cross*

PRAYER. *Father of wisdom, help me to accept all earthly misfortunes with the sure knowledge that good will come from them. Let me never despair but trust in Your Providence that governs all things.*

What profit does a man show who gains the whole world and destroys himself in the process?
—Mk 8:36

APR.
15

REFLECTION. Many are those who gain a victory over cities and castles yet fail to overcome themselves and their enemies—the world, the flesh, and the devil.

Hence, we can say that they do not possess any real benefits. — *St. Catherine of Siena*

PRAYER. *Lord of Hosts, enable me to fight continually against evil of all kinds. Let me rely on Your grace to carry off the victory and store up spiritual riches for heaven.*

I did not come to condemn the world but to save it. —Jn 12:47

APR.
16

REFLECTION. There is a unique remedy for the ills of society.

It consists in returning to Christian living and clinging to Christian institutions.

— *Pope Leo XIII*

PRAYER. *Lord Jesus, teach me to bring Your saving message and love to the world. In my own small way, let me change the world by giving Christian example to everyone I meet.*

APR. 17

Good is the Lord to one who waits for him, to the soul that seeks him. —Lam 3:25

REFLECTION. What delights we will find in forgetting self and seeking God!

The Saints renounced themselves in order to seek God and to look for Him alone. It is in this that we attain heaven. — *St. John Vianney*

PRAYER. *Infinite Lord, You are greater than anything we can imagine. Help me to forget self and seek only You in all my thoughts, words, and actions.*

APR. 18

Over all these virtues put on love, which binds the rest together and makes them perfect. —Col 33:14

REFLECTION. Love is the bond of life, the mother of the poor, and the teacher of the rich.

It is the nurse of orphans, the attendant of the elderly, the treasure of the indigent, and the common port of all the afflicted.

— *St. Gregory of Nyssa*

PRAYER. *Loving Father, pour out Your divine love into my heart and soul. Let me cooperate with that love and in this way strive for perfection in all virtues.*

Be like children as far as evil is concerned, but in mind be mature.
—1 Cor 14:20

APR. 19

REFLECTION. There are no artists more divine than those who know how to fashion a child's soul within themselves.

Such artists know how to draw forth the greatest divine radiance into their souls.

— *St. John Chrysostom*

PRAYER. *Heavenly Father, enable me to acquire the qualities of a child—simplicity, love, trust, and innocence. Let me avoid all duplicity, scheming, despair, and cynicism.*

From John the Baptizer's time until now the kingdom of God has suffered violence, and the violent take it by force.
—Mt 11:12

APR. 20

REFLECTION. The kingdom of heaven is certainly worth a great deal. Yet you can obtain it by giving what you are.

Give yourself and it is enough—for the merciful Lord is satisfied with that. — *St. Augustine*

PRAYER. *Almighty God, help me to do violence to my inordinate self-love and willfulness. Let me give myself wholly to You and so obtain the kingdom of heaven.*

APR. 21

[Jesus] went out to the mountain to pray, spending the night in communion with God. —Lk 6:12

REFLECTION. Withdraw to the inner chamber of your mind. Shut out all things except God and anything that may help you seek Him.

Then, after barring the door of your inner chamber, seek God. — *St. Anselm of Canterbury*

PRAYER. *Awe-inspiring God, teach me to know how to seek You in silence. From time to time, let me withdraw from the troubles of life and rest quietly in Your presence.*

APR. 22

You spread the table before me. . . . My cup overflows. Only goodness and kindness follow me all the days of my life. —Ps 23:5

REFLECTION. The Mass is the sun of the spiritual exercises and the center of religion.

It is the heart of devotion and the mystery in which God magnificently communicates His favors. — *St. Francis de Sales*

PRAYER. *God of goodness, teach me to appreciate the ineffable gift that the Mass is. Help me to make the Eucharist the summit toward which all my activity is directed and the fount from which all my strength flows.*

The Lord has eyes for the just and ears for their cry. —1 Pt 3:12

REFLECTION. A just life constitutes a song for the ears of our heavenly Father.

It is as pleasing to Him as the most beautiful prayer. — *St. Cyprian*

PRAYER. *Heavenly Father grant me the grace to live justly in all my activities. Let my life be ever pleasing to You on earth and obtain eternal life for me in heaven.*

Like golden apples in silver settings are words spoken at the proper time. —Prv 25:11

REFLECTION. Good books are true friends that are always with us but never nag. They speak to us but do not weary us.

They are silent when we want them to be, and they annouce great truths without dissembling. Finally, they point out our faults and weaknesses but do not displease us.

— *St. John Chrysostom*

PRAYER. *God of wisdom, inspire me to read good books, those that speak of You and the faith. Help me to regard them as real friends that will bring me closer to You every day.*

APR. 25

If I go up to the heavens, you are there; if I sink to the nether world, you are present there. —Ps 139:8

REFLECTION. There is a practice that is most powerful in keeping us united with God.

That practice is the constant recollection of His presence. — *St. Alphonsus Liguori*

PRAYER. *Omnipresent Lord, grant that I may be ever mindful of Your presence all around me. Help me to maintain a loving union with You amid the activities of my daily life.*

APR. 26

Comfort and upbuild one another as indeed you are doing. —1 Thes 5:11

REFLECTION. If on any particular day we do nothing more than give a little joy to a neighbor, that day will not be wasted.

For we have succeeded in giving comfort to an immortal soul. — *Bl. Contardo Ferrini*

PRAYER. *God of all consolation, teach me to put all my trust in You. Let me then go out and offer my neighbor Christian consolation in every tribulation.*

Through [Jesus] let us continually offer God a sacrifice of praise, that is, the fruit of lips which acknowledge his name. —Heb 13:15

APR.
27

REFLECTION. The hour has sounded for joyful chants: *Alleluia*

Let us praise God with our life, with our voice, with our heart, and with our deeds.

— *St. Augustine*

PRAYER. *Heavenly Father, help me to give You constant praise in my heart. At the same time, let this attitude bear fruit in my life—producing truly Christian deeds.*

After I have been with you all this time, you still do not know me? — Jn 14:8

APR.
28

REFLECTION. Jesus Christ is very little known by those who claim to be His friends.

We observe them seeking in Him not His sorrows but their own consolation.

— *St. John of the Cross*

PRAYER. *Lord Jesus, let me know myself and let me know You. Grant me the grace to follow You in Your sorrows—accepting all the sorrows of my life for Your sake.*

APR. 29

I am the way, and the truth, and the life; no one comes to the Father but through me. —Jn 14:6

REFLECTION. Many want to go ahead of Christ not after Him—by laying out a way to their own specifications. They seek to serve God and obtain virtue without effort.

But they deceive themselves, for Christ is "the way." — *St. Catherine of Siena*

PRAYER. *Lord Jesus, guard me from the desire to take the easy way. Grant that I may faithfully and diligently follow the way You have traced out to the Father for us.*

APR. 30

Blest are they who have not seen and have believed. —Jn 20:29

REFLECTION. This Gospel text certainly applies to us—but only if we confirm our faith by our works.

Those truly believe who carry out in practice what they believe. — *St. Gregory the Great*

PRAYER. *Jesus, my Lord and my God, help me to believe in You with all my might. And let me translate that belief into practice by obeying Your commands every day.*

You shall set apart three cities . . . [where] a homicide may take refuge . . . to save his life when [he] unwittingly kills his neighbor.

MAY 1

—Dt 19:2-4

REFLECTION.　Seek refuge in Mary because she is the city of refuge. We know that Moses set up three cities of refuge for anyone who inadvertently killed his neighbor.

Now the Lord has established a refuge of mercy, Mary, even for those who deliberately commit evil. Mary provides shelter and strength for the sinner.　— *St. Anthony of Padua*

PRAYER.　*Lord Jesus, move me to take refuge in Your holy Mother if I am so unfortunate as to lose Your grace. Help me to flee to my city of refuge, for she will lead me to You.*

Christ . . . will give a new form to this lowly body of ours, and remake it according to the pattern of his glorified body.　—Phil 3:21

MAY 2

REFLECTION.　Our human body has acquired something great through its communication with the Word. From being mortal it has been made immortal; though it was a living body it has become a spiritual one.　— *St. Athanasius*

PRAYER.　*Heavenly Father, help me to respect my body and not subject it to sin. Let me keep it ready to receive the fullness of the new form given by Your Son in heaven.*

MAY
3
I give no thought to what lies behind but push on to what is ahead. My entire attention is on the . . . prize to which God calls me.
—Phil 3:13-14

REFLECTION. It is right that you should begin again every day.

There is no better way to complete the spiritual life than to be ever beginning it over again.
— *St. Francis de Sales*

PRAYER. *Lord Jesus, make me realize that every day is a new opportunity for grace. Help me make the most of all my opportunities—to begin anew each day.*

MAY
4
For by me your days will be multiplied and the years of your life increased.
—Prv 9:11

REFLECTION. You never think of Mary without Mary thinking of God on your behalf.

Neither do you ever praise and honor God without Mary praising and honoring God in union with you. — *St. Louis Grignion de Montfort*

PRAYER. *Heavenly Father, thank You for giving me Mary as my intercessor. Enable me to collaborate with her in praising You and in saving souls.*

If only you recognized God's gift and who it is that is asking you.
—Jn 4:10

MAY 5

REFLECTION. Oh, if only the Eucharist were better understood by Christians and more worthily and frequently received.

How copious would be the fruits of harmony, peace, and spiritual decorum that would flow therefrom for the Church and the whole world! — *Pope John XXIII*

PRAYER. *Lord Jesus, help me to have a better appreciation of the Eucharist. Let me receive it with understanding, love, and thanksgiving so that it may bear abundant fruits in me.*

At once the man's ears were opened; he was freed from the impediment and began to speak plainly.
—Mk 7:35

MAY 6

REFLECTION. The knot in his tongue was untied and he spoke plainly. You too have the tongue untied and can use it when you wish.

Why do you use it for evil rather than for good? You take care to choose among foods what you want to eat. You should be just as careful to choose what you want to say.

— *St. Augustine*

PRAYER. *Heavenly Father, help me to realize the wonderful way of communicating with others that You have given me—principally through the tongue. Let me use it for good.*

MAY 7

They signaled to their mates . . . to come and help them. These came, and together they filled the two boats. —Lk 5:7

REFLECTION. The group apostolate of Christians is very important.

Often it calls for concerted effort either in ecclesiastical communities or in various other environments.

— *Vatican II: Apostolate of the Laity, no. 18*

PRAYER. *Creator of the universe, You want Christians to work together and with others to do Your work on earth. Help me to give myself freely to any undertakings that serve to build up the Body of Christ in this world.*

MAY 8

Happy the man watching daily at my gates, . . . for he who finds me finds life, and wins favor from the Lord. —Prv 8:34-35

REFLECTION. The Blessed Virgin Mary is the mother and dispensatrix of all graces.

There is not a single servant of this great Queen who can fail to declare: "It is my devotion to Mary that accounts for the growth of everything good in me." — *St. Antoninus*

PRAYER. *Lord Jesus, inspire me to go to your holy Mother in all my difficulties. Help me to be ever devoted to her and to receive the graces I need to be with You both in heaven.*

In him who is the source of my strength I have strength for everything.
—Phil 4:13

MAY 9

REFLECTION. By myself I can do nothing, but in union with God I can do all things.

Out of love for God, I want to do all things!
— *St. Vincent Palloti*

PRAYER. *God of all might, grant that I may place myself in Your hands and never despair. Let me not shrink from even the hardest task—for with Your help I can do anything.*

Those who hear the word in a spirit of openness, retain it, and bear fruit through perseverance.
—Lk 8:15

MAY 10

REFLECTION. Engrave on your heart the words of the Lord that you hear.

For the word of God is the food of the soul and should remain in our memory.
— *St. Gregory the Great*

PRAYER. *Loving Father, teach me to take Your holy word to heart as often as I come into contact with it. Enable me to be open to it, retain it, and reap the benefits it yields.*

MAY 11

This is how you are to pray: "Our Father . . . ."
—Mt 6:9

REFLECTION. The Lord's Prayer contains mysteries . . . rich in spiritual power. Every petition and prayer we are to make is included.

It is a compendium of heavenly doctrine.
— *St. Cyprian of Carthage*

PRAYER. *Lord Jesus, enable me to appreciate the depth and power of the prayer You taught us. Teach me to pray it with full understanding so that it may be my prayer par excellence.*

MAY 12

Blest are you among women and blest is the fruit of your womb.
—Lk 1:42

REFLECTION. Do you wish to know the most intimate perfections of Jesus and the most hidden attractions of His love?

Then seek them in the heart of Mary!
— *St. Peter Eymard*

PRAYER. *Lord Jesus, keep ever before me the tried and trusted Christian motto: "To Jesus through Mary." And let me learn to seek You in her Mother's heart!*

Praised be God . . . who has bestowed on us in Christ every spiritual blessing. —Eph 1:3

MAY
13

REFLECTION. Enrich your soul in the great goodness of God:

The Father is your Table, the Son is your Food, and the Holy Spirit waits on you and then makes His dwelling in You.

— *St. Catherine of Siena*

PRAYER. *Triune God, help me to realize the ineffable blessings that You have made available to all Christians. Let me be ever more conscious of the actions of the Adorable Trinity in my life.*

Justice comes from faith, not from works. —Rom 9:32

MAY
14

REFLECTION. To do works without faith is like erecting a magnificent building on a shaky foundation. The higher the building, the greater is the fall.

Without the support of faith, good works cannot stand. — *St. Ambrose*

PRAYER. *Lord Jesus, help me to avoid the error of doing works without having a living faith. Enable me always to combine both faith and works in my everyday life.*

MAY 15

He said to the disciple, "There is your mother."

—Jn 19:27

REFLECTION. The Blessed Virgin directs to us all the acts that every mother lavishes on her children.

She loves us, watches over us, protects us, and intercedes for us. — *Pope John XXIII*

PRAYER. *Lord Jesus, let me have constant recourse to Your holy Mother Mary. Grant that I may be devoted to her who loves me and takes care of me like a true Mother.*

MAY 16

Better a lowly man who supports himself than one of assured importance who lacks bread.

—Prv 12:9

REFLECTION. The value of our life does not depend on the place we occupy.

It depends on the way we occupy that place. — *St. Theresa of the Child Jesus*

PRAYER. *Almighty God, teach me the true value of life. Help me to carry out the duties of my state in the way You wish—as a dedicated follower of Your Son Jesus.*

Let not . . . the rich man glory in his riches. —Jer 9:22

MAY
17

REFLECTION. Those who possess riches outwardly must take care not to possess them inwardly, that is, with desire.

They must eliminate everything earthly from their desires. — *St. Catherine of Siena*

PRAYER. *Heavenly Father, keep my heart from dwelling on earthly riches. Help me to seek the true, spiritual riches that You give us in Christ Jesus our Lord.*

You are the glory of Jerusalem, the surpassing joy of Israel. —Jdt 15:9

MAY
18

REFLECTION. Those who want to prevent their heart from being pervaded by the evils of earth should entrust it to the Blessed Virgin, our Lady and our Mother.

They will then regain it in heaven, freed from all evils. — *St. Francis de Sales*

PRAYER. *Lord Jesus, move me to entrust my heart and my affections to Your holy Mother. Grant that her prayers may keep me from all evil and firmly attached to You forever.*

MAY 19

Zealous for the God of all, he . . . atoned for the children of Israel.

—Sir 45:23

REFLECTION. Let us spare no effort in leading souls to God.

According to the word of St. Augustine: "Where there is no zeal, neither is there any love." — *Pope Pius XI*

PRAYER. *Loving Father, You will that all people should be saved. Help me to be zealous for the salvation of all whom I encounter by my life-witness and by my prayer.*

MAY 20

If a man . . . does what is right and just . . . he holds off from evildoing.

—Ez 45:5-8

REFLECTION. Justice can be understood in many and varied ways.

Among other things, justice is the constancy of a good will. — *St. Bernardine of Siena*

PRAYER. *God of all justice, infuse into me the true virtue of justice. Let me have a good will toward You and toward all human beings— rendering to each everything that is due each.*

Live on in me, as I do in you. **MAY**
—Jn 15:4 **21**

REFLECTION. See Christ our Lord in all human beings.

In this way, you will be filled with respect and consideration for others.

— *St. Theresa of Avila*

PRAYER. *Lord Jesus, grant me the grace to see all human beings as potential persons in whom You might dwell. And let me respect them because of You, my Lord and Redeemer.*

Those who love me I also love, **MAY**
and those who seek me find me. **22**
—Prv 8:17

REFLECTION. Blessed are those who abandon themselves into Our Lady's hands.

Their names are written in the Book of Life.

— *St. Bonaventure*

PRAYER. *Heavenly Father, make me a devoted client of Your beloved Daughter Mary. Let me entrust myself always into her hands so that she may protect me as she took care of Your Son Jesus in His infancy and childhood.*

MAY 23

Every one of us will have to give an account of himself before God. Therefore we must no longer pass judgment on one another.

—Rom 14:12-13

REFLECTION. Do not seek to pass judgment on things that do not concern you.

Our Savior does not want you to do so. He reserves this judgment to Himself.

— *St. Bonaventure*

PRAYER. *Lord Jesus, let me never take it upon myself to judge others. Enable me to leave all judgment to You, for You are the all-knowing and all-powerful Judge.*

MAY 24

Mary set out... into the hill country... where she entered Zechariah's house and greeted Elizabeth.

—Lk 1:39

REFLECTION. In the interior life and in the apostolate, let us always work with Mary.

For then everything becomes easier and more certain, quicker and more delightful.

— *St. Louis Grignion de Montfort*

PRAYER. *Lord Jesus, help me to labor hard in the Christian apostolate. Teach me to work always with Your holy Mother so that I may obtain the best fruits from this work.*

78

You are badly misled because you fail to understand the Scriptures.

—Mt 22:29

REFLECTION. The whole series of the Divine Scriptures is interpreted in a fourfold way.

We should ascertain what everlasting truths are intimated therein, what deeds are narrated, what future events are foretold, and what commands or counsels are contained therein. — *St. Bede the Venerable*

PRAYER. *Heavenly Father, teach me how to read Your wonderful words in Scripture with true understanding. Let me adhere always to the interpretation given by Your Holy Church.*

It is your special privilege to take Christ's part—not only to believe in him but also to suffer for him.

—Phil 1:29

MAY 26

REFLECTION. The greatness of our God must be tested by the desire we have for suffering for His sake. . . .

Bear the cross and do not make the cross bear you! — *St. Philip Neri*

PRAYER. *Lord Jesus Christ, let me be closely united with You in all things. Grant that I may carry my cross willingly—because of You and in union with You.*

MAY 27

The spirit of the Lord shall rest upon him: a spirit of wisdom and understanding.
—Is 11:2

REFLECTION. Those who are led by the Holy Spirit have a right concept of everything.

Hence, many unlettered people enjoy such knowledge more than the wise.

— St. John Vianney

PRAYER. *Father of every good gift, send forth Your Spirit upon me with His sevenfold gifts. Grant that I may see everything with Your eyes and always act according to Your will.*

MAY 28

The Spirit of the Lord shall rest upon him: . . . a spirit of knowledge.
—Is 11:2

REFLECTION. The Holy Spirit leads us like a mother.

He leads His child by the hand . . . , as a sighted person leads a blind person.

— St. John Vianney

PRAYER. *Lord Jesus, grant me Your Spirit with His gift of knowledge. May this gift enable me to discern Your teaching and distinguish between good and evil from day to day.*

The Spirit of truth... remains with you and will be within you. **MAY**
—Jn 14:17 **29**

REFLECTION. The Holy Spirit does not remain inactive in us: He wipes away sins, purifies hearts, revivifies the tepid, and enlightens the ignorant.

His inspirations suggest to us what we ought and what we ought not to do. There exists an infinite variety of His communications.

— *St Anthony of Padua*

PRAYER. *Come, Holy Spirit, fill the heart of Your servant and kindle in me the fire of Your love.*

A man was giving a large dinner and he invited many. —Lk 14:16 **MAY**
30

REFLECTION. I am afraid when Jesus passes by. For His passing by means salvation if we respond to it but is a reason for condemnation if we pay no attention to it.

Every invitation on the part of Jesus can be termed a passing by of the Lord.

— *St. Augustine*

PRAYER. *Almighty Father, enlighten my eyes and open my heart to discern Your Son's "passing by." Let me respond promptly and wholeheartedly to His invitations addressed to me every day.*

MAY 31

Mary remained with Elizabeth about three months and then returned home.
—Lk 1:56

REFLECTION. The heart of our good mother Mary is all love and mercy. She desires nothing else but our happiness.

We need only have recourse to her and we will be heard. — *St. John Vianney*

PRAYER. *Heavenly Father, let me constantly have recourse to Mary. May she lead me to the happiness of heavenly glory which You share with Your Son in the unity of the Holy Spirit.*

JUNE 1

The words I spoke to you are spirit and life.
—Jn 6:64

REFLECTION. Make sure that you never spurn the Savior's words.

They have in themselves such tremendous majesty that they can instil fear into those who have wandered from the path of righteousness, whereas they ever remain a great solace to those who heed them. — *St. Justin the Martyr*

PRAYER: *Lord Jesus, let me daily take to heart and ponder Your words. Grant that they may lead me to penance and also provide needed consolation amid the troubles of life.*

If I . . . have not love, I gain nothing.
—1 Cor 13:3

JUNE 2

REFLECTION. The first task of love is to acknowledge before God that we belong to Him. We owe our lives to Him alone.

Hence, our hearts must be free of everything that concerns anyone else. — *St. Zeno*

PRAYER. *My loving Creator, I readily acknowledge that I belong to You. Help me to keep my heart free of all earthly distractions so that I may be united to You with all my being.*

A lamp to my feet is your word, a light to my path. —Ps 119:105

JUNE 3

REFLECTION. Being, a Christian means saying "yes" to Jesus Christ.

It consists in surrendering to the Word of God and relying on it, but also endeavoring to know better and better the profound meaning of this Word. — *Pope John Paul II*

PRAYER. *Self-revealing God, let me rely always on Your all-enlightening Word. Help me to read it often, study it diligently, ponder it well, and put it into practice in my daily life.*

JUNE 4

Say not: "I am independent. What harm can come to me now?"

—Sir 11:24

REFLECTION. Presumption is like vermin burrowing at the root of the tree of our soul.

If we do not uproot it with great care and humility, it will eventually destroy the soul.

— *St. Catherine of Siena*

PRAYER. *All-powerful God, keep me from all presumption of mind and heart. Help me to realize that I depend on You for everything and of myself I can do nothing.*

JUNE 5

He who hears You, hears me. He who rejects you, rejects me.

—Lk 10:16

REFLECTION. In her voyage across the ocean of this world, the Church is like a great ship being pounded by the waves of life's different stresses.

Our duty is not be abandon ship but to keep her on her course. — *St. Boniface*

PRAYER. *Lord, Jesus, help me to remain ever faithful to Your Church. Let me aid, build up, and defend her and remain a loyal member all my life.*

That is why her many sins are for- **JUNE**
given—because of her great love. **6**
—Lk 7:47

REFLECTION. Christians should always remember that the value of their good works is
not based on number and excellence.

Their value is based on the love for God
which prompts them to do the works.

— *St. John of the Cross*

PRAYER. *Loving Father, help me to be moti-*
vated always by true love for You. Let me not
worry so much about what I do but about why
I do it.

Through faith we perceive [under- **JUNE**
stand]. **7**
—Heb 11:3

REFLECTION. Understanding is the reward of
faith.

Therefore seek not to understand that you
may believe—but believe that you may understand.

— *Augustine*

PRAYER. *Triune God, grant that I may have a*
strong living faith in You and in Your divine
plan of salvation. Help me to believe that I may
understand and love my Christian heritage.

JUNE 8

When you have done all you have been commanded to do, say, "We are useless servants. We have done no more than our duty."

—Lk 17:9-10

REFLECTION. God is pleased with the little deeds we do in secret with no desire to be seen by others.

He takes more pleasure in these than in a multitude of grand works that we may do out of the desire to be seen by others.

— *St. John of the Cross*

PRAYER. *O Lord, help me to do faithfully what pleases You. Let me never do things just to appear great in the eyes of others.*

JUNE 9

Be on guard and pray that you may not undergo the test.

—Mt 26:41

REFLECTION. Jesus, who feared nothing, experienced fear and asked to be freed from death—although He knew it was impossible.

How much more must we persevere in prayer before temptation assails us—so that we may be freed when the test has come!

— *St. Ephrem*

PRAYER. *Heavenly Father, help me to work out my salvation in fear and trembling. Let me pray daily that I may withstand temptation and carry out Your will in all things.*

God created men in his image; . . . male and female he created them. —Gn 1:27

JUNE 10

REFLECTION. It is not true that some human beings are by nature superior and others inferior.

All human beings are equal in their natural dignity. — *Pope John XXIII*

PRAYER. *God our Creator, help me to look upon every human being as a person created in Your image and likeness. Grant that I may treat everyone the same, without favoritism or prejudice of any kind.*

There are in the end three things that last: faith, hope, and love. —1 Cor 13:13

JUNE 11

REFLECTION. Faith is the beginning and love is the end—and God is the two of them brought into unity.

Then comes everything else that makes up a Christian. — *St. Ignatius of Antioch*

PRAYER. *Almighty God, let my beginning faith end in a true love for You. And in between grant that I may attain all the other virtues that make for authentic followers of Your Son.*

87

JUNE 12

Make and keep yourself holy, because I am holy. —Lv 11:44

REFLECTION. You must be holy in the way God asks you to be holy.

God does not ask you to be a Trappist monk or a hermit. He wants you to sanctify the world and your everyday life. — *St. Vincent Palloti*

PRAYER. *Holy God, show me the path to holiness that You want me to follow. Teach me how to recognize it and help me to follow it diligently all the days of my life.*

JUNE 13

Now is the acceptable time! Now is the day of salvation. —1 Cor 6:2

REFLECTION. Regard every day as if you are then beginning for the first time.

And always act with the same fervor that you had on the first day you began.

— *St. Anthony of Padua.*

PRAYER. *Ever-living God, let me regard each day as a special gift from You to me. Enable me to be truly devoted to You and, with your unfailing help, to work out my salvation daily.*

Through the church, God's mani- **JUNE**
fold wisdom is made known.
—Eph 3:10 **14**

REFLECTION. The sight of the risen Christ helped the disciples to believe in the Church that was to follow.

In the same way, the spectacle of that Church helps to confirm our faith in the Resurrection of Christ. — *St. Augustine*

PRAYER. *Lord Jesus Christ, let Your Church be a beacon of knowledge and truth for me and for all people. Confirm my faith in Your Life, Death, and Resurrection by keeping me ever in tune with Your Church in all things.*

While everyone was asleep, his **JUNE**
enemy came and sowed weeds
through his wheat, and then **15**
made off.
—Mt 13:25

REFLECTION. We must live in constant vigilance. . . . Does this mean we must give up the possibility of sleeping? Not at all.

We cannot do without bodily sleep. What we must avoid is the sleep of the will.

— *St. John Chrysostom*

PRAYER. *Ever-vigilant Lord, let me live in constant vigilance. Grant that my will may be always completely in harmony with Your holy Will for me.*

JUNE 16 *Fathers, do not anger your children. Bring them up with the teaching and instruction befitting the Lord.* —Eph 6:4

REFLECTION. The family is the domestic Church. Parents should by word and example be the first preachers of the Faith to their children.

They should encourage their children in the vocation proper to each, carefully fostering vocations to the religious state.

— *Vatican II: The Church, no. 11*

PRAYER. *Heavenly Father, help me to take seriously my role in the domestic Church. Let me work to ensure that Christian love and harmony will always reign in my family.*

JUNE 17 *Jesus is . . . the cornerstone. There is no salvation in anyone else.* —Acts 4:11

REFLECTION. No one can advance in virtue except by following Jesus Christ.

He is the truth, the life, and the only door through whom everyone who wants to be saved must enter. — *St. John of the Cross*

PRAYER. *Father of goodness, make me realize that Jesus is the only way to You for everyone in the world. Grant that I may follow Him closely on earth and reach my heavenly home.*

How beautiful upon the mountains are the feet of him who brings glad tidings . . . announcing salvation. —Is 52:7

JUNE 18

REFLECTION. What a thrill will be yours on the last day when you hear the words of those whom you have led to heaven almost by the hand:

"These people are servants of the great God who have proclaimed the ways of salvation to us!"   — *St. John-Baptist de la Salle*

PRAYER. *Almighty God, make me a willing messenger of Your Good News of Salvation to those who do not know You. Let me be a messenger through prayer as well as through words and actions.*

I will write [my law] upon their hearts; I will be their God, and they shall be my people. —Jer 31:33

JUNE 19

REFLECTION. Things are at rest when they are in their proper place.

The proper place for the heart of a human being is the Heart of God.   — *St. Augustine*

PRAYER. *Heavenly Father, You have given me a heart that can be satisfied only by being with You. Help me to keep my heart attached to You by following Your law which is written on it.*

JUNE *Live on in my love.* —Jn 15:9

20

REFLECTION. This is what I want for you above everything else:

That you act out of pure love for Jesus Christ and out of the desire for His glory and the salvation of souls that He redeemed at such a cost.
— *St. Ignatius Loyola*

PRAYER. *Lord Jesus, help me to act always out of love for You and for the salvation of souls. Let all that I think and do and say be the result of this twofold intention.*

JUNE *In the Lord's eyes . . . a thousand years are as a day.* —2 Pt 3:8

21

REFLECTION. Everything on this earth passes away—all too quickly.

But eternity will never pass away.
— *St. Aloysius Gonzaga*

PRAYER. *Ever-living God, let me not get overly caught up in the day-to-day press of earthly affairs. Help me to keep my eye fixed on Your eternal truths and consider all things in the light of eternity.*

There is but one body and one Spirit, . . . one Lord, one faith, and one baptism. —Eph 4:4-5

JUNE 22

REFLECTION. The Lord is one and the same throughout the world.

He produces His love in His people through the Holy Spirit Whom He pours out upon all flesh. — *St. Paulinus*

PRAYER. *Heavenly Father, help me to feel at one with all Christians throughout the world. Let Your Holy Spirit pour forth Your grace into the hearts of all Christians and bring them into closer unity in the one Body of Christ.*

Treat others the way you would have them treat you. —Mt 7:12

JUNE 23

REFLECTION. Goodwill in the soul is the source of all good things and the mother of all virtues.

Those who possess it hold in their hand—without fear of losing it—all that is necessary to lead a good life. — *St. Albert the Great*

PRAYER. *Heavenly Father, grant me the true spirit of goodwill toward all. Let me be ever ready to carry out Your will and to come to the aid of all I encounter on this earthly pilgrimage.*

JUNE 24

He must increase, while I must decrease. —Jn 3:30

REFLECTION. The true secret of love consists in this:

We must forget self like St. John the Baptist and exalt and glorify the Lord Jesus.

— *St. Peter Eymard*

PRAYER. *Almighty God, help me to put my self-interests in the background. Let me seek Your interests and do everything for the honor and glory of Your Son Jesus.*

JUNE 25

May God . . . enable you to live . . . according to the spirit of Christ Jesus. —Rom 15:5

REFLECTION. Imitate Jesus, who is sovereignly perfect and sovereignly holy.

Then you will never run the danger of losing your way.

— *St. John of the Cross*

PRAYER. *Heavenly Father, enable me to put on the attitude of Your Son Jesus. Grant that I may be His follower in all things on earth so that I may follow Him to heaven.*

If you live in me, and my words stay part of you, you may ask what you will—and it will be done for you. —Jn 15:7

JUNE 26

REFLECTION. We cannot comprehend the power that a pure soul has over God.

It is not the soul that does God's will, but God Who does the soul's will.

— *St. John Vianney*

PRAYER. *Enable me to live a life of purity that will make me live in You. Let me be so united with You that whatever I might ask will be in total accord with Your will for me.*

Do you not see that your bodies are members of Christ? —1 Cor 7:15

JUNE 27

REFLECTION. All of us are united with Christ inasmuch as we have received Him Who is one and indivisible in our bodies.

Therefore, we owe the service of our members to Him rather than to ourselves.

— *St. Cyril of Alexander*

PRAYER. *Almighty God, help me to put all my faculties at the disposal of Christ so as to be His link with others and with the world. Let me give myself wholly to Him every day.*

JUNE 28

Everyone who looks upon the Son and believes in him shall have eternal life.
—Jn 6:40

REFLECTION. The Father made God visible to human beings through numerous mysteries to prevent them from losing everything—even their very lives.

For the glory of God is the living person, and the life of a person is the vision of God.

— *St. Irenaeus*

PRAYER. *Heavenly Father, let me keep alive both the natural and the supernatural life You have given me in Christ. Help me to live my earthly life to the full so that I may attain eternal life through Him.*

JUNE 29

Jesus said to Simon Peter, . . . "Feed my lambs. . . . Tend my sheep."
—Jn 21:15-16

REFLECTION. Where Peter is, there is the Church. Where the Church is, there is Jesus Christ.

Where Jesus Christ is, there is eternal salvation.

— *St. Ambrose*

PRAYER. *Lord Jesus, You left us Your Church and Your Vicar the Pope to insure our contact with You. Let me always cling to Your Church and follow its teachings with all my heart.*

Give me an account of your service.
—Lk 16:2

REFLECTION. Don't you have by your side booklets on which you enter your account each day?

In the same way, you must make an accounting every day for your conscience.

— *St. John Chrysostom*

PRAYER. *God of forgiveness, help me to make a daily examination of conscience. Teach me how to pinpoint faults, ask Your forgiveness for them, and resolve to do better in the future.*

Everyone who exalts himself shall be humbled, while he who humbles himself shall be exalted.
—Lk 18:14

REFLECTION. Observe a surprising fact. God is on high. You exalt yourself and God flees from you. You humble yourself and He comes to you.

God looks upon the humble to exalt them, but He regards the proud from afar to abase them.

— *St. Augustine*

PRAYER. *Almighty Father, whenever I seek to take pride in what I do, remind me of the way things really are. The only good I have comes from You; all that is mine is my weakness.*

JULY 2

Continually we carry about in our bodies the dying of Jesus, so that in our bodies the life of Jesus may also be revealed. —2 Cor 4:10

REFLECTION. The passible and temporal life of Jesus in His Mystical Body—that is, in Christians—has not yet reached completion.

It is being completed from day to day in each true Christian, and it will be fully completed only at the end of time. *— St. John Eudes*

PRAYER. *Heavenly Father, imprint on my mind that my task, like that of all Christians, is to build up Christ's Body on earth. Let me do whatever furthers this task and shun whatever hinders it.*

JULY 3

You are not to spend what remains of Your earthly life on human desires but on the will of God. —1 Pt 4:2

REFLECTION. Have a genuine sorrow for the slightest amount of time that you waste.

This means any time that you do not use to show your love for God. *— St. John of the Cross*

PRAYER. *Lord of time, forgive me for the time I have wasted in the past. Help me from now on to use all the time You give me to serve You in the way that You wish.*

Live as free men but do not use your freedom as a cloak for vice. . . . Live as servants of God.
JULY 4
—1 Pt 2:16

REFLECTION. God has placed good and evil in our power and has given us full freedom of choice.

He does not keep back the unwilling, but he embraces the willing. — *St. John Chrysostom*

PRAYER. *Sovereign Lord, thank You for the great gift of freedom You have bestowed on me. Grant that I may always use my freedom to serve and glorify You.*

If your enemy is hungry, feed him; . . . by doing this you will heap coals of fire upon his head.
JULY 5
—Rm 12:20

REFLECTION. We should love and feel compassion for those who oppose us, rather than abhor and despise them.

For they harm themselves and do us good. They adorn us with crowns of everlasting glory while they invite God's anger against themselves. — *St. Anthony Zaccaria*

PRAYER. *God of goodness, grant me the grace to return good toward those who do evil to me. Let me realize that they are Your instruments for fashioning me into the person You want me to be for all eternity.*

JULY 6

You will receive all that you pray for, provided you have faith.

—Mt 21:22

REFLECTION. A great faith merits great graces from the Lord.

The more things your trust dares to ask of the Lord, the more you will receive.

— *St. Bernard*

PRAYER. *Lord Jesus, grant me a strong faith and an unwavering trust in You. Help me especially in times of trial when everything appears bleak, You seem far away, and I am afraid.*

JULY 7

Whatever you do, work at it with your whole being. Do it for the Lord.

—Col 3:23

REFLECTION. We do not cease praying so long as we continue to do good.

The prayer of the heart and of good deeds has more value than the prayer of the lips.

— *St. Augustine*

PRAYER. *Dear God, move me to make a morning offering to You each day. Grant that all my deeds during the day may be a devout continuation of my prayer begun in the morning.*

I bear with all of this for the sake of those whom God has chosen.
—2 Tm 2:10

JULY 8

REFLECTION. Patience has distinctive qualities that discourses do not possess.

All who bear their cross with patience eloquently proclaim Jesus Christ.

— *St. Alphonsus Liguori*

PRAYER. *Heavenly Father, teach me to be patient under the crosses that come my way. Let my silent example speak volumes to others and lead them to faith in Your Son Jesus.*

Because the loaf of [Eucharistic] bread is one, we, many though we are, are one body, for we all partake of the one loaf.
—1 Cor 10:17

JULY 9

REFLECTION. In the Eucharist, all is love. Jesus comes to us and dwells in us.

In doing so, He teaches us how we are to love one another. — *St. Augustine*

PRAYER. *Most loving Father, grant that every Eucharistic Celebration may unite me more closely to Your Divine Son. May it also unite me to all Christians and help me to show greater love for them every day.*

101

JULY 10

Everyone who grows angry with his brother shall be liable to judgment. —Mt 5:21

REFLECTION. The sin of anger-impatience has a unique aspect.

It presents us with the greatest foretaste of hell in this life. — *St. Catherine of Siena*

PRAYER. *Lord Jesus, help me to curb my anger no matter what the circumstances. Teach me to remain calm and to strive to return good for evil in all inflammatory situations.*

JULY 11

Do not grow slack but be fervent in spirit; he whom you serve is the Lord. —Rm 12:11

REFLECTION. There exists an evil fervor, a bitter spirit, which divides us from God and leads us to hell.

Similarly, there is a good fervor which sets us apart from evil inclinations and leads us toward God and eternal life. — *St. Benedict*

PRAYER. *Loving Father, grant me to have a true fervor in Your service. Let me never tire of following Your Son's example and avoiding evil.*

Let your speech be always gra-cious and in good taste, and strive to respond properly to all who ad-dress you. —Col 4:6

JULY 12

REFLECTION. Remain at peace regarding whatever is said or done in conversations.

If it is good, you have something for which to praise God. If it is bad, you have something in which to serve God by turning your heart away from it. — *St. Francis de Sales*

PRAYER. *Lord God, let my conversations always be for the good of my soul and the souls of others. Teach me how to turn evil conversations to good and how to remain untouched by them.*

Not on bread alone is man to live but on every utterance that comes from the mouth of God. —Mt 4:4

JULY 13

REFLECTION. Meditate daily on the words of Your Creator.

Learn the Heart of God in the words of God, that your soul may be enkindled with greater longings for heavenly joys.

— *St. Gregory the Great*

PRAYER. *Heavenly Father, inspire me to meditate on Your holy words every day. Let them confer on me consolation for my past life, strength for my present life, and hope for my future life with You in heaven.*

JULY 14

Eye has not seen, ear has not heard, nor has it so much as dawned on man what God has prepared for those who love him.
—1 Cor 2:9

REFLECTION. The happiness to which I aspire is greater than anything on earth.

Therefore, I regard with extreme joy whatever pains and sufferings may befall me here.
— *St. Camillus de Lellis*

PRAYER. *Heavenly Father, keep my mind fixed on the surpassing joys stored up for me in heaven. And let me be willing to put up with all sufferings and pains that may come upon me.*

JULY 15

[God] imparts to [human beings] an understanding heart.
—Sir 17:5

REFLECTION. Do all your actions in accord with the right light of your reason.

In all things, seek your salvation, the edification of others, and the praise and glory of God.
— *St. Bonaventure*

PRAYER. *God of Reason, grant me the gift of right reasoning and Christian understanding. Let me act always in accord with the dictates of that reason and so be pleasing to You.*

I was [the Lord's] delight day by day.
—Prv 8:30

JULY 16

REFLECTION. So pleasing to God was Mary's humility that He was constrained by His goodness to entrust to her the Word, His only Son.

And it was that dearest Mother who gave Him to us. — *St. Catherine of Siena*

PRAYER. *Heavenly Father, let me always have recourse to the Mother of Your Son. May she intercede for me before Your Divine Majesty so that I may be a true follower of Your Son.*

Thoroughly wash me of my guilt. . . . For I acknowledge my offense.
—Ps 51:4-5

JULY 17

REFLECTION. Confession has been called the gate of heaven.

Through this gate the penitents are led to kiss the feet of the Divine Mercy. And they rise filled with heavenly grace.

— *St. Anthony of Padua*

PRAYER. *Merciful God, let me make frequent use of the wonderful sacrament of forgiveness You have given us. Grant that my sins may be pardoned and I may grow in Your grace.*

105

JULY 18

Owe no debt to anyone except the debt that binds us to love one another.
—Rm 13:8

REFLECTION. It is a fact that people are always well aware of what is due them.

Unfortunately, they remain oblivious of what they owe to others. — *St. Francis de Sales*

PRAYER. *Lord Jesus, let me not be so concerned with what others owe me. Help me to give to everyone what I owe them—especially the debt of love that You asked of us.*

JULY 19

O Lord, you have probed me and you know me.
—Ps 139:1

REFLECTION. Our true worth does not consist in what human beings think of us.

What we really are consists in what God knows us to be. — *St. John Berchmans*

PRAYER. *All-knowing God, let me strive always to see myself as You see me rather than as others do. Grant that, with Your help, I may grow into the person that You want me to be for eternity.*

Receive my instruction in prefer- **JULY**
ence to silver, and knowledge
rather than gold. —Prv 8:10 **20**

REFLECTION. Read attentively the book of purity that is Mary, written entirely by the finger of God.

Read the holiness, the love, the kindness, the humility—in short, read the *vast fullness* of all the virtues. — *St. Thomas of Villanova*

PRAYER. *Lord Jesus, help me to learn from Your holy Mother how to lead a Christian life. Let me strive to imitate the virtues she exhibited, for she was Your imitator on earth.*

In accord with Scripture, Christ **JULY**
did not please himself. —Rm 15:3 **21**

REFLECTION. The greatest gift that we can receive from God in the present world is this:

To know how, to desire, and to be able to conquer self by renouncing our own will.

— *St. Francis of Assisi*

PRAYER. *Heavenly Father, teach me how to discern Your will, how to follow it, and how to make it my own in all things. For in this lies true happiness both in this world and in the next.*

107

JULY 22

Each of us has received God's favor in the measure in which Christ bestows it.
—Eph 4:7

REFLECTION. God is forever bestowing visitations, gifts, and graces upon us.

What tongue can express the great many and various ways in which God does this not only for many people but for every single person!
— *St. Catherine of Siena*

PRAYER. *Lord Jesus, I thank You for the countless graces You have poured down on me from my birth. Help me to cooperate with Your grace at every moment, so that my works will not be done in vain.*

JULY 23

My command to you is: love your enemies, pray for your persecutors.
—Mt 5:44

REFLECTION. We must show love for those who do evil to us and pray for them.

Nothing is dearer or more pleasing to God than this.
— *St. Bridget*

PRAYER. *God of love, grant me the great grace to show love and forgiveness for those who do evil to me. Let me at least be able to pray for their salvation, won for them by Jesus.*

108

He who pursues . . . kindness will
find life and honor. —Prv 21:21

JULY 24

REFLECTION. We can be excused for not being always gay, for we are not masters of gaiety so as to have it when we wish.

But we cannot be excused for not being good, agreeable, and gracious, because this is always in the power of our will.

— *St. Francis de Sales*

PRAYER. *God of all goodness, teach me how to pursue goodness and kindness in all my actions. Let me never tire of showing goodness to all people out of love for You.*

Refrain from arrogant and false
claims against the truth.
—Jas 3:14

JULY 25

REFLECTION. Christians must aspire to be—with and through Christ—witnesses to the world of the truth that frees and saves us.

They must therefore be educated in the cult of the truth both in words and in actions.

— *Pope Paul VI*

PRAYER. *God of all truth, grant that I may love the truth and be wholly dedicated to it. Keep me far from all falsehood and dissembling of any kind.*

JULY 26 *All who believe ... have eternal life in him.*
—Jn 3:15

REFLECTION. Faith is in no way a burden or a yoke imposed on human beings. Far from it!

Faith is an immense benefit because it commences life in us even on this earth.

— *St. Thomas Aquinas*

PRAYER. *Heavenly Father, thank You for giving me the gift of faith. Help me to remain firm in my faith throughout my life and to strive to increase it day by day.*

JULY 27 *I am the bread of life. ... This is the bread that comes down from heaven for a man to eat and never die.*
—Jn 6:48-50

REFLECTION. How sad it is when those who have food before them let themselves die of hunger!

Take your food—the loving Lord Jesus, who was crucified for us. — *St. Catherine of Siena*

PRAYER. *Heavenly Father, let me never go hungry for spiritual food. Help me to receive Your Son often in Communion, so that I may be brought together with You in the union of the Holy Spirit.*

He has put all things under Christ's feet. —Eph 1:22

JULY 28

REFLECTION. The smallest of life's events are directed by the Lord.

Creatures are intruments, but it is the hand of Jesus that directs all.

— *St. Theresa of the Child Jesus*

PRAYER. *Lord Jesus, You have dominion over the whole earth and everything in it. Enable me to see Your guiding and loving hand behind all events and to accept each as coming from You for my good.*

The heavens declare the glory of God, and the firmament proclaims his handiwork. —Ps 19:2

JULY 29

REFLECTION. Learn to love the Creator in His creation, the Worker in His work.

Don't be so fascinated by things created that you forget the One Who created all of them.

— *St. Augustine*

PRAYER. *Almighty God, help me to love You in Your creatures—both living and nonliving. Let me realize that no matter how marvelous is Your creation, You are infinitely more marvelous and lovable.*

111

JULY 30

On the way of duty I walk, along the paths of justice, granting wealth to those who love me.

—Prv 8:20-21

REFLECTION. Mary's grace has given glory to heaven; a God to earth, and faith to the nations.

She has conferred death on vices, order on life, and a rule on morals. — *St. Peter Chrysologus*

PRAYER. *Heavenly Father, grant me the grace to have Mary as my constant intercessor. In all difficulties let me call on her aid, for she is Your beloved Daughter.*

JULY 31

I planted the seed and Apollos watered it, but God made it grow.

—1 Cor 3:6

REFLECTION. We must work as if success depended upon us alone.

At the same time, we must be wholeheartedly convinced that we are doing nothing; it is God Who is doing everything. — *St. Ignatius Loyola*

PRAYER. *All-powerful God, let me realize that no matter what I do, it is only through You that I do it. Help me to work as if all depended on me and pray as if all depended on You.*

May the Lord . . . make you over-flow with love for one another and for all. **AUG.**
—1 Thes 3:12
1

REFLECTION. The means for attaining perfect love is to accomplish frequent acts of love.

Fire is kindled by the wood that we cast into it, and love is enkindled by acts of love.

— *St. Alphonsus Liguori*

PRAYER. *Loving Father, grant me the grace to strive after perfect love. Help me to bring forth frequent acts of love so that I may grow in this greatest of virtues.*

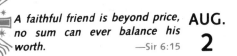

A faithful friend is beyond price, no sum can ever balance his worth. **AUG.**
—Sir 6:15
2

REFLECTION. Friendship constitutes a country for those in exile, a fortune for the poor, a remedy for the sick, and a life for the dead.

It provides pleasure for those who are well, strength for the weak, and a reward for the strong.
— *St. Augustine*

PRAYER. *Loving Father, grant me the great grace to form true Christian friendships. May my friends and I help one another to lead good lives and attain the happiness of those who serve You.*

113

AUG. 3

Anyone who loves me will be true to my word, and my Father will love him; we will come to him and make our dwelling with him.

—Jn 14:23

REFLECTION. By His grace God dwells in the just soul as in a temple, in a very close and special way.

This accounts for that bond of love which unites the soul to God and makes it rejoice in Him. — *Pope Leo XIII*

PRAYER. *Triune God, help me to prepare my soul and keep it unstained for Your sacred Indwelling. Let me never do anything that will cause me to lose grace and force You to depart from my soul.*

AUG. 4

The Father loves me for this: that I lay down my life. —Jn 10:17

REFLECTION. Martyrdom is as nothing in comparison with the Mass.

Martyrdom is the sacrifice that human beings make of their lives to God. But the Mass is the sacrifice that God makes, on behalf of people, of His body and blood. — *St. John Vianney*

PRAYER. *Lord Jesus, help me to realize that the Mass is the greatest sign of Your boundless love for me. At every Mass, let me thus offer to You my whole self, with all its joys and sorrows, success and failures.*

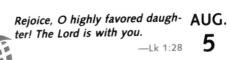

Rejoice, O highly favored daughter! The Lord is with you.

AUG.
5

—Lk 1:28

REFLECTION. The salvation of the whole world began with the "Hail Mary."

Hence, the salvation of each person is also attached to this prayer.

— *St. Louis Grignion de Montfort*

PRAYER. *Lord Jesus, let the great prayer to Your holy Mother be on my lips morning, noon, and night. Enable me to say it especially at the hour of my death—for she will insure my salvation.*

My grace is enough for you, for in weakness power reaches perfection.

AUG.
6

—2 Cor 12:9

REFLECTION. The value and the cost of grace is its interior unction which recollects us in God.

An interior grace is worth more than a thousand external graces. Our virtues and our devotion have life only through the recollection that animates them and unites them to God.

— *St. Peter Eymard*

PRAYER. *Father of all gifts, pour down on me Your inner grace and make me truly recollected in You. May all my outward activities be the result of Your grace and obtain more grace for me.*

115

AUG.
7

Though my father and mother forsake me, yet will the Lord receive me.
—Ps 27:10

REFLECTION. If you want Christ to love you and help you, you must love Him and always endeavor to please Him.

Do not waver in your purpose, because even if all the Saints and every single creature were to abandon you, He will always be near you, no matter what your needs may be. — *St. Cajetan*

PRAYER. *Lord Jesus, let me love You above all things and ever remain united with You. Help me to do always the things that are pleasing to You.*

AUG.
8

He who feeds on my flesh and drinks my blood has life eternal.
—Jn 6:54

REFLECTION. God's glory and goodness consist above all in the emanations of His tenderness.

Hence, those who approach the Divine Sacrament obtain God's glory much more than those who abstain from receiving it.

— *St. Thomas Aquinas*

PRAYER. *Lord Jesus Christ, never let me abstain from receiving You in Holy Communion out of laziness or disinterest. Help me to receive Communion often and with ever-increasing devotion.*

116

It is precisely in this that God proves his love for us: that while we were still sinners, Christ died for us.
—Rm 5:8

AUG. 9

REFLECTION. A soul is a great treasure and a rich deposit.

For the eternal Wisdom, Who cannot be deceived, regarded it as more precious than His own Blood.
— *St. Bernard*

PRAYER. *Heavenly Father, let me never forget the incomparable value of my immortal soul. Help me to be willing to die rather than risk doing anything to lose that soul.*

The fruit of the Spirit is love, joy, peace, patient endurance, kindness, generosity, faith, mildness and chastity.
—Gal 5:22

AUG. 10

REFLECTION. The sun penetrates crystal and makes it more dazzling.

In the same way, the sanctifying Spirit indwells in souls and makes them more radiant. They become like so many powerhouses beaming grace and love around them.
— *St. Basil*

PRAYER. *Heavenly Father, let me be ever ready to cooperate with the graces given by Your indwelling Spirit. Grant that I may bring forth the fruits You desire.*

AUG. 11

[Wisdom] is the refulgence of eternal light, the spotless mirror of the power of God. —Wis 7:26

REFLECTION. Every day, look into the spotless mirror that is Jesus Christ, and study well your reflection.

In that way, you may adorn yourself, mind and body, with every virtue. — *St. Clare of Assisi*

PRAYER. *Lord Jesus, help me to dwell often on the manner in which I am following You. Let me strive each day to become more and more like You in all things.*

AUG. 12

A gracious woman wins esteem. . . . A kindly man benefits himself. —Prv 11:6-7

REFLECTION. Do not chase after all kinds of knowledge, enlightenment, and understanding in the hope of gaining the hearts of others.

You will gain those hearts more surely by showing openness and graciousness to them.

— *St. John Chrysostom*

PRAYER. *Gracious Lord, help me to show openness and graciousness to others. In this way let me win over their hearts on earth and gain their souls for eternity.*

[God] gave us . . . a birth to an imperishable inheritance . . . which is kept in heaven for you.

AUG. **13**

— 1 Pt 1:3-4

REFLECTION. You have within you everything that you need to purchase the kingdom of heaven.

Joy will be purchased by your sorrow, rest by your labor, glory by your humiliation, and eternal life by your passing death.

— *St. Augustine*

PRAYER. *Loving Father, teach me how to make every event on earth lay up treasures for me in heaven. Help me to endure sorrows, labors, humiliations, and death willingly so as to attain heaven.*

Mine are counsel and advice; mine is strength; I am understanding.

AUG. **14**

—Prv 8:14

REFLECTION. When we dedicate ourselves to Mary, we become instruments in her hands just as she is an instrument in God's hands.

Let us then be guided by her for she will provide for the needs of body and soul and overcome all difficulties and anxieties.

— *St. Maximilian Kolbe*

PRAYER. *Dear Jesus, in all my trials and difficulties, let me have recourse to You through Your holy Mother. Grant that she may comfort me and lead me to You.*

119

AUG. 15

Those that sow in tears shall reap rejoicing. —Ps 126:5

REFLECTION. Mary sowed much in tears while on earth, and now she is reaping much in heavenly joy.

The same will be true for us. The more spiritual victories we attain while on earth, the more we will receive in heaven. — *St. Bernard.*

PRAYER. *Heavenly Father, grant me Your grace to obtain daily spiritual victories over myself, the world, and the devil. Let me be faithful as Mary was and so share her glory with You.*

AUG. 16

If you show favoritism, you commit sin and are convicted by the law. —Jas 2:9

REFLECTION. Do not show favor only to relations and kin, or to the most eminent—whether they are leaders or the wealthy or neighbors or citizens of the same country.

Show favor to all who come to you. By fulfilling your duty in this way, you will reach the highest state of happiness.

— *St. Stephen of Hungary*

PRAYER. *Just Father, help me to overcome all tendencies to show favoritism in my life. Let me treat all persons as brothers and sisters in Christ and work and pray for their salvation.*

This is my blood, the blood of the covenant, to be poured out in behalf of many for the forgiveness of sins. **AUG. 17**
—Mt 26:28

REFLECTION. The Eucharist may be termed a perpetual Calvary.

Without it how many times God's wrath would have erupted on our heads!
— *St. Peter Eymard*

PRAYER. *Heavenly Father, make me realize that the Eucharist is the memorial of Christ's action that freed me of my sins. Help me to participate devoutly in every Eucharist and obtain the grace to avoid sin.*

Well done You are an industrious and reliable servant. . . . Come share your master's joy! **AUG. 18**
—Mt 25:21

REFLECTION. In God's house we must try to accept whatever job he gives us: cook, kitchen boy, waiter, stable boy, or baker.

For we know that our reward depends not on the job itself but on the faithfulness with which we serve God. — *John John Paul I*

PRAYER. *Heavenly Father, help me to accept the task you have given me to do in life. Let me be faithful to it all my days and be able to attain Your eternal reward in heaven.*

AUG. 19

You are my children, and you put me back in labor pains until Christ is formed in you. —Gal 4:19

REFLECTION. There is only one reason for us to be living on earth.

We are to bear, manifest, sanctify, glorify, and cause to live and reign in us the name, life, qualities and perfections, dispositions, and inclinations, and virtues and actions of Jesus.

— *St. John Eudes*

PRAYER. *Heavenly Father, impress upon my mind and heart that I must be conformed to Your Son in all things. Let me imitate Him so completely that I may truly be "another Christ."*

AUG. 20

Hold fast to ... a good conscience. Some men, by rejecting the guidance of conscience, have made shipwreck of their faith. —1 Tm 1:19

REFLECTION. A good conscience is a treasury of riches.

Indeed, what greater riches can there be—or what can be sweeter—than a good conscience?

— *St. Bernard*

PRAYER. *All-knowing God, let me be able to stand in your presence with a good conscience. Help me to avoid anything that would sully my conscience and do all I can to remain united with You.*

You are sad for a time; but I shall see you again; then your hearts will rejoice with a joy no one can take from you. —Jn 16:22

AUG. 21

REFLECTION. Catholics are part of the Church Militant. They struggle and they suffer for the triumph of Christ.

They must never lose sight of their Divine Model, so that their trials will be turned into joy. — *St. Pius X*

PRAYER. *Jesus, Lord of Sorrows, enable me to struggle and suffer in union with You. Let me keep ever before me the joy that will follow upon these passing sufferings.*

My fruit is better than gold, yes, than pure gold, and my revenue than choice silver. —Prv 8:19

AUG. 22

REFLECTION. Mary is the stem of the beautiful flower on which the Holy Spirit rests with the fullness of His gifts. Hence, those who want to obtain the seven gifts of the Spirit must seek the flower of the Holy Spirit on the stem [Mary].

We go to Jesus through Mary, and through Jesus we find the grace of the Holy Spirit.

— *St. Bonaventure*

PRAYER. *Heavenly Father, You made Mary the Spouse of the Holy Spirit. Help me through Mary and Jesus to reach the Spirit and obtain His surpassing gifts.*

123

AUG. 23

It is in Christ . . . that we have been redeemed and our sins forgiven, so immeasurably generous is God's favor [grace] to us.

—Eph 1:7

REFLECTION. If only we would learn how great it is to possess divine grace and how many riches it has within itself, how many joys and delights

We would devote all our concern to winning for ourselves pains and afflictions in order to attain the unfathomable treasure of grace.

— *St. Rose of Lima*

PRAYER. *God is all goodness, keep ever in my mind the surpassing riches of Your grace. Grant that I may devote all my efforts to cooperating with that grace and growing in it day by day.*

AUG. 24

[God] chose to reveal his Son to me, that I might spread among the Gentiles the good tidings concerning Him. —Gal 1:16

REFLECTION. No matter where you may be or where you may be working, make sure the world will be renewed upon contact with you.

Make the Lord more present to human beings and the Gospel more known and loved by them.

— *Pope Paul VI*

PRAYER. *Heavenly Father, teach me to imitate Your divine Son in my life. Grant that by my presence as well as by my deeds I may bring Christ and His message to everyone I meet.*

The servant of the Lord ... must be an apt teacher, patiently and gently correcting those who contradict him. AUG. 25 —2 Tm 2:24-25

REFLECTION. All who undertake to teach must be endowed with deep love, the greatest patience, and, most of all, profound humility. They must perform their work with earnest zeal.

Then, through their humble prayers, the Lord will find them worthy to become fellow workers with Him in the cause of truth.

— *St. Louis*

PRAYER. *Dear Lord, help me to teach others about You by my example as well as my words. Grant that I may spread Your truth and Your light wherever I go.*

Give thanks to God the Father always and for everything in the name of our Lord Jesus Christ. AUG. 26 —Eph 5:20

REFLECTION. We must never fail to thank our Lord after we have received some sign of goodness, some benefit, from Him.

For God loves grateful hearts and heaps blessings on them. — *St. Mary Euphrasia*

PRAYER. *Heavenly Father, thank You for all the graces and blessings you have bestowed on me from my birth. Help me to show my gratitude by using all Your gifts for Your glory and the betterment of human beings.*

AUG.
27

My human life . . . is a life of faith in the Son of God, who loved me and gave himself for me.

—Gal 2:20

REFLECTION.   The crucifix is an open book that all can read.

The crucifix is an infinite declaration of love.

— *St. Catherine of Siena*

PRAYER.   *Lord Jesus Christ, inspire me to read the Crucifix often. Grant that I may return thanks and love to You for Your great love for me.*

AUG.
28

Let us love in deed and in truth and not merely talk about it.

—1 Jn 3:18

REFLECTION.   Love, and do what you will. If you are silent, be silent out of love. If you speak, speak out of love. If you censure, censure out of love. If you forbear, forbear out of love.

But love in your heart. Nothing but good can spring from that source.   — *St. Augustine*

PRAYER.   *Heavenly Father, grant me the gift of your love so that whatever I do I may do out of that love. Let me love, and do what I will—that is, love in deed and in truth.*

You will receive power when the **AUG.**
Holy Spirit comes down on you;
then you are to be my witnesses... **29**
even to the ends of the earth.

—Acts 1:8

REFLECTION.   The holy People of God share in Christ's prophetic office.

They spread abroad a living witness to Him, especially by means of a life of faith and love and by offering to God a sacrifice of praise.

— *Vatican II: The Church, no. 12*

PRAYER.   *Lord Jesus, help me to share in Your prophetic office through the Holy Spirit. Let my entire life bear powerful witness to You and bring peoples true knowledge of Your name.*

Without warning a violent storm **AUG.**
came up on the lake, and the boat
began to be swamped by the **30**
waves. Jesus was sleeping. . . .

—Mt 8:24-24

REFLECTION.   It is impossible to go through life without trials, because trials are the natural proofs of faith. Like watchful mariners, we should be sure to awaken the Pilot of our ship.

Those who allow themselves to be overcome by fear while in the company of Jesus deserve to be reproached by Him. For all who are united with Him cannot perish. — *St. Ambrose*

PRAYER.   *Jesus, in every trial let me come to You with confidence. Make me realize that You are always present and ready to respond to my call.*

127

AUG.
31

He told them a parable on the necessity of praying always and not losing heart. —Lk 18:1

REFLECTION. *Pray always*—here is what these words mean:

Either prayer must always be on our *lips* to ask for some grace. Or it must be in our *heart* in the desire for this grace. Or it must be in our *works*, which are a preparation for efficacious prayer. — *St. Bonaventure*

PRAYER. *Heavenly Father, teach me the value of praying always. Grant that every event of my life may be the occasion for praying—with my lips, my heart, or my works.*

SEPT.
1

They devoted themselves to the apostles' instruction and the communal life, to the breaking of bread and the prayers. —Acts 2:24

REFLECTION. When the Church prays in her Liturgy, it is Christ Who prays.

For the Church prays in Christ, and Christ prays in the Church; the Body prays in the Head, and the Head in the Body. — *St Augustine*

PRAYER. *Glorious Lord, help me to pray the Liturgy in union with Christ for Your glory. At every Eucharist, let me consciously adore and thank You, make reparation to You, and present my petitions before You.*

Better is childlessness with virtue for immortal is its memory.
—Wis 4:1

SEPT. 2

REFLECTION. Just as the stars are the ornament of the firmament, so the virtues are the ornament and the light of the soul.

Virtue is, so to speak, heaven in our heart.
— *St. John Climacus*

PRAYER. *All-holy God, grant me the grace to attain the Christian virtues. Let my whole life revolve around them in such a way that I may also radiate them to others.*

Since the creation of the world . . . God's eternal power and divinity have become visible, recognized through the things he has made.
—Rm 1:20

SEPT. 3

REFLECTION. God is within all things, but not included; outside all things, but not excluded.

God is above all things, but not beyond their reach.
— *St. Gregory the Great*

PRAYER. *Lord of creation, grant me the grace to see You in all things and in all places on earth. Help me to seek and reach You in all the events I experience and all the persons I encounter every day of my life.*

129

SEPT.
4
Each one has his own gift from God. —1 Cor 7:7

REFLECTION. All the faithful of every state and condition are armed with a great deal of wondrous means of salvation.

They are thus called by the Lord—each in his or her own way—to attain that perfection of holiness with which the heavenly Father is perfect. — *Vatican II: Constitution on the Church, no. 11*

PRAYER. *Heavenly Father, help me to be holy in the way that You have laid out for me. Let me carry out the duties of my state in life to the full and so attain the holiness proper to me.*

SEPT.
5
It is by way of admonition that [the Lord] chastises those who are close to him. —Jdt 8:27

REFLECTION. Suffering out of love for God is a signal favor, but we do not realize this.

For we thank God for prosperity and take no heed that afflictions would be a much greater grace. —*St. Joseph of Cupertino*

PRAYER. *Compassionate Lord, teach me to regard all suffering as something allowed by You to make me more like Your Son Jesus. Help me to accept in this light whatever suffering may come to me.*

130

What we shall later be has not yet come to light. We know that when it comes to light we shall be like him.
—1 Jn 3:2

SEPT.

6

REFLECTION. To love is to be transformed into what we love.

To love God is therefore to be transformed into God. — *St. John of the Cross*

PRAYER. *Heavenly Father, grant me Your grace to love You and to be ever more like You day after day. Enable me at the end of my life to be totally conformed to You and to see You as You are.*

Come by yourselves to an out-of-the-way place and rest a little.
—Mk 6:30

SEPT.

7

REFLECTION. Whosoever looks into murky and agitated waters cannot see his own countenance.

If you want the face of Christ to appear in your countenance, pause, recollect your thoughts in silence, and shut the door of the soul to the noise of exterior things.

— *St. Anthony of Padua*

PRAYER. *Lord Jesus, teach me to pause often during my active life and recollect myself. Let me put away the problems of life and commune with You in prayer and meditation.*

SEPT. 8

Forsake her not, and she will preserve you; love her, and she will safeguard you.
—Wis 4:6

REFLECTION. Go to Mary and sing her praises, and you will be enlighted.

For it is through her that the true Light shines on the sea of this life. — *St. Ildephonsus*

PRAYER. *Lord Jesus, help me to have recourse often to Your holy Mother Mary. Grant that she may obtain from You all the graces I need to serve You in this world and give eternal glory to You in the next.*

SEPT. 9

I am not seeking my own will but the will of him who sent me.
—Jn 5:30

REFLECTION. What good is it for you to give God one thing when He asks for something else?

Discover what God wants and do it. Your heart will be happier than if your own desire had been fulfilled. — *St. John of the Cross*

PRAYER. *Heavenly Father, let me strive— through constant prayer and careful reflection—to know Your will for me. Then help me to offer You what You desire rather than what I want.*

You have mercy on all, ... and you overlook the sins of men that they may repent. —Wis 11:23 **SEPT. 10**

REFLECTION. Our Lord bowed His head at death, so that He might give the kiss of peace to His beloved ones.

And we give a kiss to God every time our heart is filled with repentance and love.

— *St. Augustine*

PRAYER. *Lord Jesus, by Your death and Resurrection You take away the sins of the world. Grant me true repentance for all my sins and a firm resolution never more to commit them.*

The man who feeds on my flesh and drinks my blood remains in me and I in him. —Jn 6:55 **SEPT. 11**

REFLECTION. If we were to receive the Most Blessed Sacrament with great faith and ardent love, it would take only one reception for us to become spiritually rich.

By the same token, what an incalculable spiritual effect would a large number of such devout Communions have on us!

— *St. Theresa of Avila*

PRAYER. *Lord Jesus, help me to receive You in Communion with ever more faith and love. Let me strive to obtain the greatest spiritual benefits possible from each reception of this Blessed Sacrament.*

133

SEPT. 12 *[Share] your bread with the hungry, and [shelter] the oppressed and the homeless.* —Is 58:7

REFLECTION. Deprive yourself of some part of your substance, and give it wholeheartedly to the poor. God will restore it to you not only in the next life but even in the present one.

Love the poor, and be happy to associate with them often. — *St. Francis de Sales*

PRAYER. *Heavenly Father, help me to give some part of whatever I possess to those who have less. Let me strive to give help in any way I can to those who are less fortunate than I am.*

SEPT. 13 *It is [Christ] who is head of the body, the Church.* —Col 1:18

REFLECTION. Never separate yourself from the Church. No institution has the power of the Church.

The Church is your hope. The Church is your salvation. The Church is your refuge.

— *St. John Chrysostom*

PRAYER. *Lord Jesus, grant me the grace to adhere to the Church all my life. Let me encounter You in her Sacraments on earth and so possess eternal life with You in heaven.*

He who does not take up his cross and come after me is not worthy of me. —Mt 10:38

SEPT. 14

REFLECTION. The cross is the greatest gift God could bestow on His Elect on earth. There is nothing so necessary, so beneficial, so sweet, or so glorious as to suffer something for Jesus.

If you suffer as you ought, the cross will become a precious yoke that Jesus will carry with you. — *St. Louis Grignion de Montfort*

PRAYER. *Lord Jesus, impress upon me that without a cross on earth there will be no crown in heaven. Help me to bear my cross daily for You as You bore Your Cross for me and all human beings.*

Near the cross of Jesus there stood his mother. —Jn 19:25

SEPT. 15

REFLECTION. During the entire course of her life, the Blessed Virgin Mary, Mother of God, never deviated in the slightest from the precepts and examples of her Divine Son.

This was true both in the most sweet joys Mary experienced and in the cruel sufferings she underwent, which made her the Queen of Martyrs. — *Pope Pius XII*

PRAYER. *Lord Jesus, in all my sorrows let me imitate the fidelity of Your holy Mother. And through her intercession grant me Your consolation here and eternal joy in heaven.*

135

SEPT.
16

Your will be done on earth as it is in heaven.
—Mt 6:10

REFLECTION. We must carry out the will of God rather than our own. This is what we pledge to do in the "Our Father," which we recite every day.

What a travesty it would be if after praying that God's will be done we should carry out that will halfheartedly and only because we are obliged to do so! — *St. Cyprian of Carthage*

PRAYER. *Heavenly Father, let me curb my own desires and strive to discover Your will for me. Help me to do that will wholeheartedly in all things, for You have my best interests at heart.*

SEPT.
17

Work with anxious concern to achieve your salvation.
—Phil 2:12

REFLECTION. You have been created for the glory of God and your own eternal salvation. . . .This is your goal; this is the center of your life; this is the treasure of your heart.

If you reach this goal, you will find happiness. If you fail to reach it, you will find misery. — *St. Robert Bellarmine*

PRAYER. *Heavenly Father, teach me to do everything for Your honor and glory. Grant me the grace to work out my salvation with anxious concern each day of my life.*

How slow you are to believe all that the prophets have announced! Did not the Messiah have to undergo all this so as to enter into his glory? —Lk 24:25-26

SEPT.
18

REFLECTION. Christ's love and obedience had abased Him to the death of the Cross.

Therefore, Christ was raised by God to the glory of the Resurrection. — *St. Thomas Aquinas*

PRAYER. *Lord of glory, stamp indelibly on my mind that without the Cross there is no crown. Help me to fashion an eternal crown of glory out of the little crosses that come my way each day.*

REFLECTION. Let us brace ourselves with strong energy against the incitements of evil habits.

By so doing, we can often turn those evil habits to the account of virtue.

— *St. Gregory the Great*

PRAYER. *Almighty God, let me be ever mindful that You can draw good out of evil. Help me to fight against my evil tendencies and turn them into occasions for strengthening virtues.*

SEPT. 20

Behold the rainbow! Then bless its Maker, for majestic indeed is its splendor.

—Sir 43:11

REFLECTION. Whenever our eyes feast on a spectacular scene—such as a magnificent landscape, or a splendid sunset, or a beautiful star-studded sky—let us realize that it is only a pale reflection of the Divine Beauty.

Let us then bless the Lord as being the sole source of all good. — *St. Theresa of Avila*

PRAYER. *Almighty Creator, teach me to appreciate the wondrous things You have made. Grant me the grace to see You in each of them and give You the praise and glory owed You.*

SEPT. 21

The word of the Lord endures forever. Now this "word" is the gospel which was preached to you.

—1 Pt 1:25

REFLECTION. Everything that Christ willed to have us read about His actions and words He caused to be written down by the Evangelists as if by His own hands.

Thus readers of the Gospels will receive what is told them as if they saw the Lord Himself writing it with His own hand.

— *St. Augustine*

PRAYER. *Lord Jesus, help me to see the Gospel as Your word to me today. Grant me the grace to meditate on it daily and to live my life in accord with its teachings.*

The whole body grows ... with the proper functioning of the members joined firmly together by each supporting ligament.

SEPT.
22

—Eph 4:16

REFLECTION. The foundation and origin of the whole apostolate of the Church is Christ, sent by the Father.

Hence, it is evident that the fruitfulness of the apostolate of the laity depends on the vital union with Christ. — *Vatican II: Laity, 4*

PRAYER. *Lord Jesus, help me to be a contributing member of Your Mystical Body on earth. Let everything I do be done in union with You and serve to build up Your Body.*

[God] has loved us and has sent his Son as an offering for our sins.

SEPT.
23

—1 Jn 4:10

REFLECTION. God's love for us has no equal. It infinitely surpasses the love nature has imprinted in the hearts of parents.

We can be certain that whatever such a Father sends us is for our good.

— *St. Alphonsus Rodriguez*

PRAYER. *Loving Father, let me believe firmly in Your love for me despite all the trials that may come my way. Help me to cling to the thought that You want only what is best for my eternal welfare.*

SEPT. 24

Make fast friends with a man while he is poor. —Sir 22:23

REFLECTION. Every virtue can attract the friendship of others to us. For every virtue is a good, and anything good is lovable to all and renders lovable all who possess it.

Friendship blossoms, grows, and is strengthened in the measure that virtue develops.
— *St. Thomas Aquinas*

PRAYER. *Lord Jesus, our true Friend, help me to cultivate virtues and so gain friends. In turn, let my friends also pursue virtues—making our friendship closer and bringing us all into Your eternal Friendship in heaven.*

SEPT. 25

May Christ dwell in your hearts through faith. —Eph 3:17

REFLECTION. Bear Christ in heart, mind, and will.

Bear Him in your mind by His teaching. Bear Him in your will by your observance of the Law. Bear Him in your heart by the Holy Eucharist.
— *Pope Pius XII*

PRAYER. *Heavenly Father, let me be a true bearer of Christ, Your Son, by doing always the things that are pleasing to Him. Help me to bear witness to Him in the world for the salvation of souls.*

The love of Christ impels me.
— 2 Cor 5:14

REFLECTION. The Holy Eucharist does not merely place within us the habits of grace and virtue.

It also impels us to act, in accordance with the words of St. Paul the Apostle: "The love of God impels us." — *St. Thomas Aquinas*

PRAYER. *Lord Jesus, with every Communion that I receive let me be geared toward Christian action. Help me to cooperate with Your grace and practice all the virtues.*

When peaceful stillness compassed everything . . . , your all-powerful word from heaven's royal throne bounded. —Wis 18:14

REFLECTION. Silence exists so that we might speak to God.

And it is in silence that God communicates His graces to us. — *St. Vincent de Paul*

PRAYER. *Heavenly Father, teach me to appreciate the value of silence in my life. Let me set aside a few silent moments each day for thinking about You and speaking with You.*

SEPT.

28

There will . . . be more joy in heaven over one repentant sinner than over ninety-nine righteous who have no need to repent.

—Lk 15:7

REFLECTION. Nothing makes God happier than a person's amendment of life, conversion, and salvation.

This is why He sent His only Son to this earth. — *St. Gregory Nazianzen*

PRAYER. *Holy God, help me to amend my life constantly and be sincerely converted to You. Let me seek Your interests rather than my own and be ever more closely united with You.*

SEPT.

29

The angel Gabriel was sent from God to a town of Galilee named Nazareth, to a virgin. —Lk 1:26-27

REFLECTION. Angels take different earthly forms at the bidding of their master, God.

They thus reveal themselves to human beings and unveil the Divine Mysteries to them.

— *St. John Damascene*

PRAYER. *God of all Wisdom, You direct the ministry of angels and of human beings. Grant that the angels who always minister to You in heaven may defend us during our life on earth.*

In your fight against sin you have not yet resisted to the point of shedding blood. —Heb 12:4

SEPT. 30

REFLECTION. Martyrdom does not consist only in dying for one's faith.

Martyrdom also consists in serving God with love and purity of heart every day of one's life. — *St. Jerome*

PRAYER. *Dear Lord, let me offer You all my daily struggles against sin and evil. Grant me the strength to resist even to the shedding of blood if it should be required of me.*

Everyone who exalts himself shall be humbled, and he who humbles himself shall be exalted.
—Lk 14:11

OCT. 1

REFLECTION. The true and only glory is the glory that will last forever.

In order to attain it, we do not need to do spectacular deeds. We need merely hide ourselves from the eyes of others and even from ourselves. — *St. Theresa of the Child Jesus*

PRAYER. *God of glory, impress on me the value of humility as a means of attaining true glory. Help me to humble myself in my own eyes as well as in the eyes of all.*

143

OCT. 2

To his angels he has given command about you, that they guard you in all your ways. —Ps 91:11

REFLECTION. The Angels are the shepherds of our souls. Not content with bringing our messages to God, they also bring God's messages to us.

They nourish our souls with their delightful inspirations as well as their Divine communications. — *St. John of the Cross*

PRAYER. *Lord of the heavenly hosts, let Your Angels ever watch over me in this life. Grant that they may also bring my prayers before You and confer Your grace upon me.*

OCT. 3

If we love one another God dwells in us, and his love is brought to perfection in us. —1 Jn 4:12

REFLECTION. The love that we bear toward creatures must be a spiritual one and founded on God alone. Then the love of God will grow in our souls to the same extent that our love grows.

The more our hearts remember our neighbor, the more they will also recall God. These two loves grow side by side. — *St. John of the Cross*

PRAYER. *Heavenly Father, increase my love for You every day. At the same time, let this love overflow into love for all other people in the world, who have been created and blessed by You.*

REFLECTION. Do you want to know one of the best ways to win over people and lead them to God?

It consists in giving them joy and making them happy. — *St. Francis of Assisi*

PRAYER. *Lord Jesus, grant me Your grace to serve You with gladness. Then enable me to lead others to You through the joy and gladness that I dispense to them.*

A patient man is better than a warrior, and he who rules his tempter, than he who takes a city.

—Prv 16:32

OCT.
5

REFLECTION. Human beings must have patience with one another.

And the good people are those who bear the defects of others in the best way.

— *St. Francis de Sales*

PRAYER. *Long-suffering God, help me to have patience with others and with myself in all circumstances. Let me imitate Your long-suffering in whatever may befall me every day.*

OCT. 6

Sacrifice or oblation you wished not, but ears open to obedience you gave me. —Ps 139:7

REFLECTION. By your work you show what you love and what you know.

When you observe true obedience with prudence and enthusiasm, it is clear that you pick the most delightful and nourishing fruit of Divine Scripture.

— *St. Bruno*

PRAYER. *Heavenly Father, let me realize that You guide our lives through legitimate authority in every area. Help me to be obedient to the rules for my state in life and so be obedient to Your will for me.*

OCT. 7

Open your petals, like roses planted near running waters. —Sir 39:13

REFLECTION. To discover whether people are of God, I have found no better way than the following.

Observe whether they say the Hail Mary and the Rosary. — *St. Loius Grignion de Montfort*

PRAYER. *Lord Jesus, let me realize that the Rosary is nothing more than a meditation on Your Holy Mysteries in company with Your Mother. Help me to recite my Rosary daily, if possible.*

May our Lord Jesus Christ... console your hearts and strengthen them for every good word and work. —2 Thes 2:16-17

OCT. 8

REFLECTION. Jesus knows how to comfort us. So when you are desolate, leave creatures behind.

Come to the tabernacle, and you will always find strength and consolation.

— *St. Peter Eymard*

PRAYER. *Lord Jesus, let me frequently have recourse to You in the Blessed Sacrament. O Sacrament most holy, O Sacrament divine, all praise and all thanksgiving be every moment thine!*

If your brother should commit some wrong against you, go and point out his fault. —Mt 18:15

OCT. 9

REFLECTION. Those who want to work for moral reform in the world must seek the glory of God before everything else.

They must wait for God's help in this difficult and necessary undertaking, for He is the source of all good. — *St. John Leonardi*

PRAYER. *Almighty God, help me to work for moral reform in the world in everything I do. But let me rely on Your grace so that I may effect a reform that is true rather than one that is purely my own.*

OCT.
10

Stern as death is love, relentless as the nether world is devotion.
—Song 8:6

REFLECTION.   Love can supply for a life that is cut short.

God does not look at time, for He is eternal. He looks only at love.

— *St. Theresa of the Child Jesus*

PRAYER.   *Father, let me have the true love that You intend for me. Grant that because of the great love I have for You I may then gain eternity with You.*

OCT.
11

I heard the voice of the Lord saying, Whom shall I send? . . . "Here I am," I said; "send me!"   —Is 6:8

REFLECTION.   You ask what you might offer to God. Offer yourself!

What does God expect from you—except yourself?

— *St. Augustine*

PRAYER.   *Help me to discern through prayer and meditation what You truly want of me. Then enable me to offer it to You—and indeed to offer myself and all I have to You.*

How deep are the riches and the wisdom and the knowledge of God! —Rm 11:33

OCT. 12

REFLECTION. With heartfelt love let us sing of our Eternal Father's Providence—all-wise, all-powerful, and all-gentle.

O the depth of the riches, the wisdom, and the knowledge of God! — *St. Frances de Sales*

PRAYER. *All-provident Father, teach me to trust wholeheartedly in Your loving care. Help me to see that all that takes place is for my ultimate good, no matter how it may appear.*

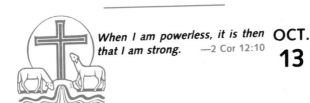

When I am powerless, it is then that I am strong. —2 Cor 12:10

OCT. 13

REFLECTION. Never trust in yourselves alone, saying: "I'm strong and I have no fear that anything or anyone can make me fall."

For love of God, stay away from such a misguided way of thinking! — *St. Catherine of Siena*

PRAYER. *Lord Jesus, keep me from pride and vanity of all kinds. Let me distrust myself in all things and put all my trust in You—without hesitation or reservation.*

OCT.
14

It is God who, in his good will toward you, begets in you any measure of desire or achievement.

—Phil 2:13

REFLECTION. Let us ask God's help before doing anything.

If we acted in this way, we would perform wonders, for it would be God acting always in us.
— *St. Peter Eymard*

PRAYER. *Heavenly Father, let me call upon Your help before undertaking to do anything in my life. Grant that I may be so united with You that Your grace me always bring forth good fruit.*

OCT.
15

God is greater than our hearts.

—1 Jn 3:20

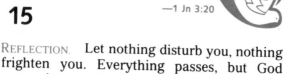

REFLECTION. Let nothing disturb you, nothing frighten you. Everything passes, but God never changes. Patience obtains everything.

Those who possess God lack for nothing. God alone is enough. — *St. Theresa of Avila*

PRAYER. *Heavenly Father, let me remain calm amid all the difficulties of life. Help me to preserve my union with You, which is the one thing necessary in this world.*

None of those who cry out, "Lord, Lord," will enter the kingdom of God but only the one who does the will of my Father. —Mt 7:21

OCT.
16

REFLECTION. Virtue does not consist in making splendid resolutions.

It consists in carrying out those resolutions and producing good fruits.

— *St. Margaret Mary Alacoque*

PRAYER. *Lord Jesus, help me to put all my good resolutions into effect. Grant that I may always bring forth good fruits from my union with God.*

Live according to what you have learned and accepted. —Phil 4:9

OCT.
17

REFLECTION. It is better to say nothing and be a Christian than to speak and not be one.

It is good to teach, if we practice what we preach. — *St. Ignatius of Antioch*

PRAYER. *Heavenly Father, grant that I may believe what I have learned and practice what I believe. Help me to lead a truly Christian life in addition to speaking about it.*

151

OCT.
18

Out of fear I went off and buried your thousand silver pieces [talents] in the ground.... His master exclaimed: "You worthless, lazy lout." —Mt 25:25-26

REFLECTION.   God has given to each of us the talents to sow His words and gather up the fruit of souls.

Let us therefore put those talents to work and not bury them in the ground.

— *St. Catherine of Siena*

PRAYER.   *Lord Jesus, grant me the grace to make use of the talents You have given me. Let me put them to work for the salvation of souls and for Your eternal glory.*

OCT.
19

Do not grow lazy, but imitate those who, through faith and patience, are inheriting the promise.

— Heb 6:12

REFLECTION.   If we are united inwardly with the Son of the living God, we also bear His likeness outwardly by our continual practice of heroic goodness.

We do so especially by a patience reenforced by courage that does not complain either secretly or publicly.   — *St. John de Brébeuf*

PRAYER.   *Long-suffering God, help me to practice patience in doing good. No matter what may occur, let me face each day with quiet courage and without complaint.*

Name something that you have not received. If, then, you have received it, why are you boasting as if it were your own? —1 Cor 4:7

OCT. 20

REFLECTION. The reason why God is such a great Lover of humility is that He is a great Lover of truth.

Humility is in fact truth, while pride is nothing but lying. — *St. Vincent de Paul*

PRAYER. *God of truth, help me to realize that everything I have is from you. Let me show my gratitude by always using it in accord with Your holy will.*

In Christ Jesus neither circumcision nor the lack of it counts for anything; only faith, which expresses itself through love. —Gal 5:6

OCT. 21

REFLECTION. To believe in God—for Christians—does not mean simply to believe that God exists, nor merely to believe that He is true.

It means to believe by loving, to believe by abandoning oneself to God, uniting and conforming oneself to Him. — *St. Anthony of Padua*

PRAYER. *Heavenly Father, grant me an operative faith, a faith that will move mountains. Let me show that faith by lively deeds and by conforming myself to Your will in all things.*

153

OCT. 22

The Church of the living God [is] the pillar and bulwark of truth.

—1 Tm 3:15

REFLECTION. The Church has the following characteristic qualities.

She overcomes when she is attacked. She is understood when she is disputed. And she grows greater when she is abandoned.

— *St. Hilary of Poitiers*

PRAYER. *Heavenly Father, let me always cling to Your Church for she is my best contact with You. Grant that I may never depart from this pillar of truth—the prolongation of Your Son Jesus in the world.*

OCT. 23

You are the salt of the earth.

—Mt 5:13

REFLECTION. Remove from your lives the filth and uncleanness of vice.

Your upright lives must make you the salt of the earth for yourselves and for the rest of humankind.

— *St. John of Capistrano*

PRAYER. *Heavenly Father, enable me both to practice and to preach Your Message to all those I meet. Grant that—in accord with Your Son's mandate—I may be the salt of the earth.*

I have been most zealous for the Lord, the God of hosts.

OCT. 24

—1 Kgs 19:14

REFLECTION. Truly zealous persons are also those who love, but they stand on a higher plane of love.

The more they are inflamed by love, the more urgently zeal drives them on.

— *St. Anthony Claret*

PRAYER. *Lord God of Hosts, grant me a holy zeal for You based on a love that is true. May everything I do contribute to Your greater glory and bring others to You.*

Carnal allurements, enticements for the eye, the life of empty show—all these are from the world.

OCT. 25

—1 Jn 2:16

REFLECTION. What does it mean to renounce all that we have and all that we desire?

It means we renounce the world and all that it contains.

— *St. Augustine*

PRAYER. *Triune God, help me to give up that world which is opposed to You. Let me be willing to renounce everything I possess and everything I want—so that I may possess You forever.*

OCT. 26

O children, listen to me; instruction and wisdom do not reject!
—Prv 8:32-33

REFLECTION. Let Mary never be far from your lips and from your heart.

Following her, you will never lose your way. Praying to her, you will never sink into despair. Contemplating her, you will never go wrong. — *St. Bernardine of Siena*

PRAYER. *Lord Jesus, help me to have continual recourse to Your holy Mother. Grant that she may watch over me as she lovingly watched over You in Your childhood at Nazareth.*

OCT. 27

The love of God has been poured out in our hearts through the Holy Spirit who has been given to us.
—Rm 5:5

REFLECTION. One and the same love embraces both God and neighbor.

This love is the Holy Spirit, Who is Divine Love. — *St. Anthony of Padua*

PRAYER. *Come, Holy Spirit. Fill the heart of Your faithful one and enkindle in me the fire of Your love. Divine Guest of my soul, abide in me and grant that I may abide in You.*

The mouth of the just man tells of wisdom and his tongue utters what is right. —Ps 37:30

OCT. 28

REFLECTION. Truthful persons do not keep silent when it is the time for speaking out.

They keep silent only when it is the time to be silent. But then their very silence cries out!
— *St. Catherine of Siena*

PRAYER. *God of truth, grant me the wisdom and the courage to speak the truth without fear of others. Let me be silent only when it is Your will for me to do so.*

Learn a lesson from the way the wild flowers grow. They do not work; they do not spin. —Mt 6:28

OCT. 29

REFLECTION. In telling us to learn a lesson from the wild flowers that do not sow, Jesus is not encouraging us to avoid working.

He is simply forbidding us to become overly anxious about things. — *St. John Chrysostom*

PRAYER. *Lord Jesus, help me to have the right attitude toward work. Let me make it an integral part of my Christian life by offering it to Your service and that of my neighbor.*

OCT.
30
You are light in the Lord....
Light produces every kind of
goodness. —Eph 5:8-9

REFLECTION. Goodness has the same relationship to the human heart that a magnet has to iron.

Goodness has the power to attract the heart.
— *St. Thomas Aquinas*

PRAYER. *God of light, let my heart be ever attracted to goodness rather than to evil. Help me to live as a child of light, devoted to You every day of my life.*

OCT.
31
I urge you not to indulge your carnal desires. By their nature they wage war on the soul. —1 Pt 2:11

REFLECTION. The virtue of chastity does not mean that we are insensible to the urge of concupiscence.

It means that we subordinate it to reason and the law of grace, by striving wholeheartedly after what is noblest in human and Christian life. — *Pope Pius XII*

PRAYER. *Heavenly Father, enable me to subordinate the urges of concupiscence to reason and grace. Grant that I may lead a noble and pure Christian life.*

You are fellow citizens of the **NOV.**
saints and members of the house-
hold of God. —Eph 3:19

1

REFLECTION. A ray of light enables us to see the dust that is in the air. In the same way, the lives of the Saints show up our defects.

If we fail to see our faults, it is because we have not looked at the lives of holy men and women. — *St. Anthony of Padua*

PRAYER. *Heavenly Father, help me to love and respect Your Saints. Grant me to obtain an example from their way of life, fellowship in their communion, and aid through their intercession.*

The souls of the just are in the **NOV.**
hands of God. —Wis 3:1

2

REFLECTION. What great power the holy souls in purgatory have over the heart of God!

If we realized this fact and averted to all the graces that we can gain through their intercession, these souls would not be so forgotten.
— *St. John Vianney*

PRAYER. *God, our Creator and Redeemer, grant to the souls in purgatory the remission of their sins. And may their prayers also be of benefit to me and all my dear ones.*

NOV. *Set your heart on what pertains to*
3 *higher realms where Christ is seated at God's right hand.*

—Col 3:1

REFLECTION. Not all of us understand spiritual values as well as we should, nor do we give them a proper place in our lives.

Many of us, strongly attracted by sin, look upon such values as of no importance or ignore them altogether. — *Pope John XXIII*

PRAYER. *Lord Jesus, help me to appreciate spiritual values and give them the first place in my heart. Grant that I may always seek them first and remain forever united with you.*

NOV. *Of you my heart speaks; you my*
4 *glance seeks; your presence, O Lord, I seek.*

—Ps 27:8

REFLECTION. If a tiny spark of God's love already burns in you, do not expose it to the wind, for it may get blown out.

In other words, avoid distractions as much as you can. Stay quiet with God. Do not spend your time in useless chatter.

— *St. Charles Borromeo*

PRAYER. *Almighty God, help me to seek You and speak with You often. Let me strive to avoid outer distractions and concentrate on Your message and Your will for me.*

Give to Caesar what is Caesar's, but give to God what is God's.

—Mt 22:21

NOV. 5

REFLECTION. There are no better citizens—whether in peace or in war—than Christians who are mindful of their duty.

Such persons must be willing to suffer all things—even death—rather than abandon the cause of God or of the Church. — *Pope Leo XIII*

PRAYER. *Heavenly Father, grant me a love for my country and a desire to help it as a good citizen. At the same time let me remain a faithful member of Your Church and work for her benefit.*

I acknowledge my offense, and my sin is before me always.

—Ps 51:5

NOV. 6

REFLECTION. In your daily prayer, confess your sins to God with tears and sighs.

And make a purpose of amendment of these sins for the future. — *St. Benedict*

PRAYER. *God of mercy, teach me to make a daily examination of conscience with a firm resolution of amendment. Help me to avoid all sins in the future—and especially my most outstanding faults.*

NOV. *Keep your conscience clear.*

7 —1 Pt 3:16

REFLECTION. Conscience and reputation are two different things.

Your conscience depends on you, whereas your reputation depends on your neighbor's estimation of you. — *St. Augustine*

PRAYER. *All-knowing God, help me to keep my conscience clear in Your sight. Grant that I may never give in to human respect—but strive always to do what I know is right.*

NOV. *Why look at the speck in your brother's eye when you miss the plank in your own?* —Mt 7:3

8

REFLECTION. It is very easy for us to find fault with others.

But it is very hard for us to isolate and correct our own faults. — *St. Francis de Sales*

PRAYER. *Lord Jesus, help me to avoid finding fault with others. Let me strive instead to discover my own faults and seek to correct them as fast as I can.*

The temple of God is holy, and you are that temple. —1 Cor 3:17

NOV. 9

REFLECTION. When Christ came, He banished the devil from our hearts, in order to build in them a temple for Himself.

Let us then do what we can with His help, so that our evil deeds will not deface that temple.
— *St. Caesarius of Arles*

PRAYER. *Lord Jesus, help me to be a true temple of God: Father, Son, and Holy Spirit. Grant me the grace to keep this temple holy and pleasing to You all my days.*

You shall love the Lord your God. . . . This is the greatest and first commandment. The second is like it: "You shall love your neighbor as yourself."
—Mt 22:37-38

NOV. 10

REFLECTION. If we love our neighbor, we automatically love God as well.

For it is in the unity of this twofold love that God has constituted the fullness of the Law and the Prophets.
— *St. Leo the Great*

PRAYER. *Loving Father, help me to realize that love is the most powerful force in the world. Let me love You and my neighbor because of You.*

NOV. 11

Render constant thanks; such is God's will for you in Christ Jesus.
—1 Thes 5:18

REFLECTION. Ingratitude is the enemy of our immortal souls.

Ingratitude empties our souls of merit, scatters their virtues, and deprives them of graces.

— *St. Bernard*

PRAYER. *Almighty Father, help me to show gratitude to You for all the good things You have done for me. Let me also be grateful to all those who help me on my earthly pilgrimage to Your heavenly Kingdom.*

———————————

NOV. 12

Cast me not off in my old age; as my strength fails, forsake me not.
—Ps 71:9

REFLECTION. Do not wait for old age to offer yourself to God.

Offer him the flower of your youth, which will be pleasing to Him and which He will accept with the greatest of love.

— *St. Catherine of Siena*

PRAYER. *God of all ages, grant that I may give myself to You at every age of life—youth, adulthood, and old age. Then in my old age continue to take care of me.*

One may toil and struggle and drive, and fall short all the same.
—Sir 11:11

REFLECTION. Be very careful to preserve your health.

The devil employs a trick to deceive good souls. He incites them to do more than they are able, in order that they may no longer be able to do anything. — *St. Vincent de Paul*

PRAYER. *Heavenly Father, help me to use moderation in everything I do. Let me never try to do more than I am able and more than You require of me—but rather to do Your will alone.*

If anyone would serve me, let him follow me.
—Jn 12:26

NOV. **14**

REFLECTION. Do you wish to receive grace upon grace and to grow from virtue to virtue?

Then make the Stations of the Cross every day. — *St. Bonaventure*

PRAYER. *Lord Jesus, help me to make the Stations of the Cross frequently, and even daily if possible. Grant that in following You by this devotion I may obtain the grace and courage to follow You in all the events of my daily life.*

165

NOV. 15

Blessed are the single-hearted for they shall see God. —Mt 5:8

REFLECTION. The surest and quickest way to attain perfection is to strive for purity of heart.

Once the obstacles have been removed, God finds a clear path and does wonders both in and through the soul.

PRAYER. *Heavenly Father, give me a heart that knows and seeks nothing but You. Grant me the grace to keep my heart free from all worldly cares and intent on spiritual things.*

NOV. 16

If you wish to enter into life, keep the commandments. —Mt 19:17

REFLECTION. The Ten Commandments are completed by the Evangelical Precepts of justice and love.

Together these constitute the framework for individual and collective survival.

— *Pope John XXIII*

PRAYER. *Lord of eternal life, grant me the grace to follow Your Commandments and Evangelical Precepts of love and justice. Help me to base my earthly life on Your Law and thus enter into eternal life.*

Death is swallowed up in victory. "O death, where is your victory? O death, where is your sting?"
—1 Cor 15:54-55

NOV. 17

REFLECTION. Human beings are by nature afraid of death; but there is a startling fact about this.

Those who have put their faith in the Cross despise even what is naturally fearful. For the sake of Christ, they are not afraid of death.

— *St. Athanasius*

PRAYER. *Lord Jesus, help me to put all my trust in You and face death without fear. Grant me the grace to remain faithful to You till death and to attain eternal life with You.*

Avoid greed in all its forms. A man may be wealthy, but his possessions do not guarantee him life.
—Lk 12:15

NOV. 18

REFLECTION. We all know that we must be innocent of greed.

However, it is an excellent rule for us to banish greed even beyond the reach of scandal.

— *St. Bernard*

PRAYER. *All-generous God, help me to avoid all kinds of greed for the goods of this world. Teach me to amass spiritual riches which will ensure unending life with You in heaven.*

NOV. 19

Endure your trials as the disciples of God, who deals with you as sons. —Heb 12:7

REFLECTION. Suffering is like a kiss that Jesus hanging from the Cross bestows on persons whom He loves in a special way.

Because of this love He wants to associate them in the work of the Redemption.

— *St. Bonaventure*

PRAYER. *Loving Lord, help me to look upon suffering as a sign of Your special love for me. Let me accept it and suffer in union with You for my salvation and that of the whole world.*

NOV. 20

If you honor [the holy day] by not following your ways [or] seeking your own interests . . . you shall delight in the Lord. —Is 58:13-14

REFLECTION. Perfection does not consist in lacerating the body.

Rather it consists in curbing our perverse self-will. — *St. Catherine of Siena*

PRAYER. *Heavenly Father, teach me to curb my wayward self-will. Instead of subjecting my body to my own whims, may I concentrate on doing Your will in all things rather than my own.*

Sincere are all the words of my mouth . . .; all of them are plain to the man of intelligence.

NOV. 21

—Prv 8:8-9

REFLECTION. What a wondrous book is the heart of Mary!

Blessed are those who read with intelligence what is written therein, for they will learn the science of salvation. — *St. John Eudes*

PRAYER. *Lord Jesus, help me to contemplate the science of salvation found in Your Mother's heart. Grant that I may imitate her in all things, for she was Your perfect follower.*

Give thanks to the Lord on the harp. . . . Sing to him a new song.

NOV. 22

—Ps 33:2-3

REFLECTION. Only the "new" person can sing a new song to the Lord: the person restored from a fallen condition through the grace of God.

Let us sing a new song not with our lips but with our lives. — *St. Augustine*

PRAYER. *Heavenly Father, help me to sing to You the song of the redeemed every day. Let my whole life be an uninterrupted song of thanksgiving and praise to You.*

NOV.
23

Put on the armor of God, if you are to resist on the evil day.

—Eph 6:13

REFLECTION. Let us then serve in Christ's army, following His blameless commands with all our might.

The great cannot exist without the small, nor the small without the great. They blend together to their mutual advantage. — *St. Clement*

PRAYER. *Lord Jesus, help me to be a true member of Your spiritual army, which is Your Mystical Body. Let me treat everyone I meet as my associate in Christ and work for our mutual benefit.*

NOV.
24

I myself am the living bread come down from heaven. If anyone eats this bread, he shal live forever.

— Jn 6:51

REFLECTION. The Eucharist is the true Catholic standard for recognizing a disciple of Jesus Christ.

It is in Holy Communion that we recognize one another. — *St. Peter Eymard*

PRAYER. *Lord Jesus, grant that I may have a surpassing love for the Blessed Eucharist. Help me to be closely united with everyone who receives You in Holy Communion.*

I determined that while I was with you I would speak of nothing but Jesus Christ and him crucified.

—1 Cor 2:2

NOV. 25

REFLECTION. When we meditate on the Passion of our Lord Jesus Christ, we should manifest compassion for His sufferings.

Then we should contemplate Him with love in this state and out of love appropriate for ourselves the sufferings He endured.

— St. Paul of the Cross

PRAYER. *Father of compassion, let me learn to have compassion on my crucified Lord. Teach me to dwell on His sufferings and make them part of my life in some way each day.*

Praise and glory, wisdom and thanksgiving and honor . . . to our God forever and ever. —Rv 7:9

NOV. 26

REFLECTION. We should be ever mindful of all the benefits we have received from God during life.

Happy shall we be if we strive to thank God for them.

— St. Bernard

PRAYER. *Heavenly Father, thank You for the many marvelous gifts—both natural and supernatural—that You have bestowed on me. Let me never forget Your goodness toward me.*

NOV. 27

Let us pray and beg our Lord to have mercy on us and to grant us deliverance.
—Tb 8:4

REFLECTION. There is no holiness without the grace of God.

And this grace can be obtained by our prayer.
— *St. Pius X*

PRAYER. *God of holiness, pour down upon me all the graces I need to be a true follower of Your Son Jesus. Help me to pray often for Your saving grace.*

NOV. 28

[God] has made everything appropriate to its time.
—Eccl 3:11

REFLECTION. Each moment of our lives comes to us invested with an order from God.

And what we make of it will become part of all eternity.
— *St. Francis de Sales*

PRAYER. *Heavenly Father, let me make the most of every moment You give me. Grant that I may build up eternity with the moments You allot to me on earth.*

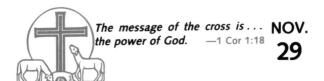

The message of the cross is . . . the power of God. —1 Cor 1:18

NOV. 29

REFLECTION. Christians must lean on the Cross of Christ just as travelers lean on a staff when they begin a long journey.

They must have the Passion of Christ deeply imbedded in their minds and hearts, because only from it can they derive peace, grace, and truth. — *St. Anthony of Padua*

PRAYER. *Lord Jesus, let me rely always on the power of Your Cross. Grant that I may attain the salvation which You won for us by Your Passion and Resurrection.*

My kingdom does not belong to this world. —Jn 18:36

NOV. 30

REFLECTION. Jesus is King because He governs souls and provides for their eternal salvation.

He is King because He leads into His eternal Kingdom all who believe and hope in Him and live in His love. — *St. Augustine*

PRAYER. *Lord Jesus, I acknowledge You as the King of the universe and ask You to exercise upon me all Your rights. Help me to offer You all my actions to obtain that all hearts may acknowledge Your Sacred Kingship.*

173

DEC.
1

Make the most of the present opportunity, for the days are evil.

—Eph 5:16

REFLECTION. Let us not allow this holy season of Advent to slip by without spiritual fruit.

It is the time of salvation; let us profit from it.
— *St. Mary Euphrase*

PRAYER. *God of mercy, teach me to live in tune with Your Liturgical Year. Help me to be filled with the sentiments proper to Advent and to prepare fittingly for the renewed birth of Your Son in my heart.*

DEC.
2

I am the companion of all who fear you.

—Ps 119:63

REFLECTION. Cultivate the friendship of others. It is the consolation of this life to find someone who is a confidant in the mysteries of our soul.

The source of Christian friendship is none other than God.
— *St. Augustine*

PRAYER. *Heavenly Father, help me to seek out truly Christian friends. Let me always be a genuine friend to them, working for their spiritual as well as material good.*

For the sake of the joy which lay before him he endured the cross.

—Heb 12:2

DEC. 3

REFLECTION. I am in a country where all the niceties of life are lacking.

But I am filled with many inner consolations. Indeed, I run the risk of crying my eyes out because of my tears of joy!

— *St. Francis Xavier*

PRAYER. *Heavenly Father, grant me the inner consolation to possess spiritual joy in all circumstances. Let me be so united with You that I will joyfully bear with all tribulations.*

I have much more to tell you, but you cannot bear it now.

—Jn 16:12

DEC. 4

REFLECTION. God knows all things and provides what is profitable for each one.

He revealed what it is to our benefit to know. But He kept secret what we are unable to bear now.

— *St. John Damascene*

PRAYER. *Lord Jesus, help me to meditate on Your Revelation every day. Grant that by learning fully what You have revealed, I may one day in heaven attain the knowledge of all that You did not reveal.*

175

DEC. 5

These ... are the festivals of the Lord which you shall celebrate at their proper time with a sacred assembly. —Lv 23:4

REFLECTION. The Eucharist is the sun of the feasts of the Church.

It sheds light on those feasts and renders them living and joyous. — *St. Peter Eymard*

PRAYER. *Lord Jesus, help me to participate in the Eucharist with true devotion throughout the year. Let me encounter You in Your Mysteries and remain united with You every day of my life.*

DEC. 6

Cast me not out of your presence, and your Holy Spirit take not from me. —Ps 51:13

REFLECTION. When the Holy Spirit is in a soul, He communicates Himself in one way or another.

We can say that He makes virtue contagious and turns a simple faithful into an apostle.

— *Bl. Claude de la Colombiere*

PRAYER. *Heavenly Father, grant that Your Holy Spirit may inspire me to be a true follower of Your Son Jesus. May He dwell in me always and keep me ever on the path of holiness.*

You ... are a "chosen race, a royal priesthood, a holy nation."

DEC. 7

—1 Pt 2:9

REFLECTION. All the children of the Church are priests. At Baptism they received the anointing that gives them a share in the priesthood.

The sacrifice that they must offer to God is completely spiritual—it is themselves.

— *St. Ambrose*

PRAYER. *Holy Father, teach me to offer myself to You with all my thoughts, words, and actions, Let me also exercise my "common priesthood" by faithful participation at Mass.*

You shall love the Lord your God with all your heart, with all your soul, with all your strength, and with all your mind.

DEC. 8

—Lk 10:27

REFLECTION. Love for Christ pierced Mary's heart in such a way that no part of it was left unkindled.

Mary thus fulfilled the first commandment of love in all its fullness and without the slightest imperfection. — *St. Bernard*

PRAYER. *Heavenly Father, help me to imitate Your immaculate Daughter Mary in her love for You. Grant me the grace to love You as much as I can all my life.*

DEC. 9

How I wish you were . . . hot or cold! But because you are lukewarm . . . I will spew you out of my mouth!
—Rv 3:15

REFLECTION. The Word of God moves swiftly. He is not won by the lukewarm nor held fast by the negligent.

Be attentive to His message and diligently follow the path God tells you to take. For He is swift in His passing. — *St. Ambrose*

PRAYER. *Lord Jesus, help me to avoid being lukewarm in my spiritual life. Grant me an ardent faith, hope, and love so that I may be zealous in following You every day.*

DEC. 10

[Jesus] said to Peter, "Put out into deep water and lower your nets for a catch."
—Lk 5:4

REFLECTION. The bark of Peter laughs at the winds and the waves.

She has the Saints as her passengers, the Cross as her mast, the Gospel teachings as her sails, the Angels as her rowers, and God as her pilot. — *St. John Chrysostom*

PRAYER. *Heavenly Father, teach me to trust Your Church as the Bark of Salvation in this world. Grant that I may work and pray to remain afloat with her amid the storms of life.*

No man should seek his own interest but rather that of his neighbor. —1 Cor 10:24

DEC. 11

REFLECTION. The law of love obliges us to love what is good for us.

But it also obliges us to love what is good for our neighbor. — *St. Francis de Sales*

PRAYER. *Father of all, help me to be truly concerned about other people who are also Your children. Grant that for Your sake I may love others as I love myself.*

Who is this that comes like the dawn . . . as awe-inspiring as bannered troops? —Song 6:10

DEC. 12

REFLECTION. Mary is an arsenal of graces and she comes to the aid of her clients.

She sustains, strengthens, and revives us by the heavenly favors that she heaps on us.

— *St. Paulinus*

PRAYER. *Lord Jesus, help me to become a devoted client of Your holy Mother Mary. Through Your grace, may I receive the spiritual strength she has promised to all her clients.*

179

DEC. 13

Do not lay up for yourselves an earthly treasure.... Store up heavenly treasure, which neither moths nor rust corrode nor thieves break in and steal. —Mt 6:19-20

REFLECTION. Let us lose nothing of what God bestows on us. Difficulties and sufferings will disappear, but the merit we acquire through our fidelity will remain forever.

Let us therefore build our eternity through all the things that pass away.

— *St. Jane Frances de Chantal*

PRAYER. *Father in heaven, teach me to store up a treasury of merits for eternity. Grant that I may use this earthly life to be the person You want me to be for eternity.*

DEC. 14

Lead a life worthy of the Lord and pleasing to him in every way.... Multiply good works of every sort. —Col 1:10

REFLECTION. Strive unceasingly to be pleasing to God and ask Him to accomplish His will in you.

Love Him with all your might; you owe Him a great deal. — *St. John of the Cross*

PRAYER. *God of power and might, let me do always the things that are pleasing to You. For You are my Greatest Benefactor and my Sole Good.*

God's bread comes down from heaven and gives life to the world.
—Jn 6:33

DEC.
15

REFLECTION. All who receive Jesus in Communion are filled with every good.

Their temptations are overcome. Their troubles are turned into joys. And their piety finds nourishment. — *St. Anthony of Padua.*

PRAYER. *Lord Jesus, help me to receive You in Communion frequently and with fervor. Grant that all my Communions may enable me to do good, avoid evil, and live always as a dedicated Christian.*

Seek after integrity, piety, faith, love, steadfastness, and a gentle spirit.
—1 Tm 6:12

DEC.
16

REFLECTION. Virtue is a very wonderful thing for us.

It is the good of life, the fruit of a clear conscience, and the peace of the innocent.

— *St. Ambrose*

PRAYER. *Heavenly Father, help me to build up virtue in my life. Let me realize that by cultivating all the virtues I will attain happiness not only in heaven but also here on earth.*

DEC. 17

My heart and my flesh cry out for the living God. —Ps 84:3

REFLECTION.   Desire to see God, be fearful of losing Him, and find joy in everything that can lead to Him.

If you act in this way, you will always live in great peace. — *St. Theresa of Avila*

PRAYER.   *Living God, let me desire to see You and make use of everything that leads to You. Grant that I may live in such a way as to gain the blessed vision of You in heaven.*

DEC. 18

We walk by faith, not by sight. —2 Cor 5:7

REFLECTION.   Faith is like a bright ray of sunlight.

It enables us to see God in all things as well as all things in God. — *St. Francis de Sales*

PRAYER.   *Heavenly Father, help me to shine the spotlight of Your faith on the world I live in. Grant that I may see You everywhere and serve You in everything.*

*Here I stand, knocking. . . . If any-
one . . . opens the door, I will
enter his house and have supper
with him.* —Rv 3:20

**DEC.
19**

REFLECTION.   Speak to Jesus and you will give
joy to His heart.

Your own heart will open up to the ray of
this Sun of Goodness like humid and chilled
flowers on a spring morning. *— St. Peter Eymard*

PRAYER.   *Lord Jesus, let me learn to open the
door to my heart to You and speak with You
daily. Let me be inundated with the warmth of
Your love and direction so that I may follow
You more closely every day.*

*You, O God, are my stronghold,
my gracious God!* —Ps 59:18

**DEC.
20**

REFLECTION.   In tribulations, turn to God with
confidence. You will obtain strength, light,
and knowledge.

In joys and successes, turn to God with fear
and sincerity. You will escape all snares and
be free of everything false.

— St. John of the Cross

PRAYER.   *Heavenly Father, let me turn to You
in good times and bad during my life. Grant
that I may always remain in loving union with
You no matter what adversity or success may
befall me.*

183

DEC. 21

God who is mighty has done great things for me, holy is his name.
—Lk 1:49

REFLECTION.   While remaining the Mother of our Judge, Mary is a mother to us, full of mercy.

She constitutes our protection. She keeps us close to Christ, and she faithfully takes the matter of our salvation into her charge.

— *St. Peter Canisius*

PRAYER.   *Heavenly Father, You have filled Mary with grace and made her a Co-Redeemer with Christ Your Son. Grant that I may have constant recourse to her and attain the salvation she helped win for the world.*

DEC. 22

A child is born to us, a son is given us; upon his shoulder dominion rests.
—Is 9:5

REFLECTION.   In adoring our Savior's birth, it is our origin that we celebrate. Christ's temporal generation is the source of the Christian people, the birth of His Mystical Body.

All of us encounter in this Mystery a new birth in Christ — *St. Leo the Great*

PRAYER.   *Heavenly Father, in celebrating the birth of Your Son on earth, let me also celebrate my birth in His Mystical Body. Grant that I may thus be brought closer to You in union with Your only Son.*

184

On coming into the world, Jesus said: . . . "I have come to do your will, O God." By one offering He has forever perfected those who are being sanctified.

DEC. 23

REFLECTION. Jesus Christ, the God-Man, was born in a manger and is spiritually reborn on the altar. He suffered on Calvary and continues to offer Himself on the altar.

In His earthly life He spread His teaching and worked miracles among the crowds. In the Eucharist, He spans the centuries and communicates Himself to all. — *St. John Chrysostom*

PRAYER. *Heavenly Father, in contemplating the birth of Your Son in time and in the Eucharist, may I ever attain a new birth.*

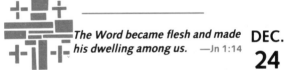

The Word became flesh and made his dwelling among us. —Jn 1:14

DEC. 24

REFLECTION. The sun's rays light up the world without separating themselves from the sun.

In like manner, the Son of God comes down to earth to enlighten us without separating himself from the Father with Whom He is entirely one. — *St. Anthony of Padua*

PRAYER. *Come Lord Jesus, and give me new courage, for I trust in Your love. By Your renewed coming at Christmas and in the Eucharist, raise me to heavenly glory*

185

DEC. 25

Mary gave birth to her first-born son and wrapped him in swaddling clothes and laid him in a manger.
—Lk 2:7'

REFLECTION. The One who is seated on the throne of heaven is laid in a stable.

A God Who is beyond access is touched by the hands of human beings!

— *St. John Chrysostom*

PRAYER. *Heavenly Father, let me welcome Your Son as my Redeemer now. Then help me to go to meet Him with confidence when He comes to be my Judge at the end of my earthly life.*

DEC. 26

God is love, and he who abides in love abides in God, and God in him.
—1 Jn 4:16

REFLECTION. Love is the source of all good things. It is an impregnable defense and the way that leads to heaven.

Those who walk in love can neither go astray nor be afraid. Love guides and protects them and brings them safely to their journey's end.

— *St. Fulgentius*

PRAYER. *Loving Father, pour forth Your love in my heart and help me always to act in accord with it. Let me be ruled by Your love in all things so that I may experience it completely with You in heaven.*

We have seen his glory: The glory of an only Son coming from the Father, filled with enduring love.
—Jn 1:14

REFLECTION. The Word is visible to the heart alone, whereas flesh is visible to bodily eyes as well.

The Word was made flesh so that we could see it, to heal the part of us by which we could see the Word. — *St. Augustine*

PRAYER. *Invisible God, help me to see Jesus made flesh as a visible reflection of You. Let me thus come to know You, be filled with love for You, and desire to be with You forever.*

Come, let us sing to the Lord; let us acclaim the Rock of our salvation.
—Ps 95:1

REFLECTION. We do not use only our voices and our lips when we sing a song.

We utter an inner song because there is in us Someone Who listens. — *St. Augustine*

PRAYER. *Heavenly Father, let me sing Your praises with all that I think, say, or do. Grant that my whole life will reflect Your abiding presence within me to everyone I encounter.*

DEC.
29

I have fought the good fight, I have finished the course, I have kept the faith. From now on a merited crown awaits me.

—2 Tm 4:7

REFLECTION. Remember how the crown was attained by those whose sufferings gave new radiance to their faith.

The whole company of saints bears witness to the unfailing truth that without genuine effort no one wins the crown.

— *St. Thomas Becket*

PRAYER. *Lord of glory, help me to attain the crown of glory You hold out to me. Grant me the grace to make a continuous and dedicated effort to lead a good life until the very end.*

DEC.
30

I have stilled and quieted my soul like a weaned child. —Ps 131:2

REFLECTION. Strive to accustom yourself to renounce the things that you have in your heart and the little satisfactions that you desire.

This is the secret that enables you to preserve peace of soul. — *St. Francis de Sales*

PRAYER. *God of peace, let me be at peace with myself and my desires. Teach me to put all my trust in You and desire only what You have willed for me.*

REFLECTION.   Be watchful and vigilant. It is by design that Jesus concealed the last day from us.

He wants us to be on the lookout for him every day of our lives.   — *St. Augustine*

PRAYER. *Lord Jesus, help me to be alert and on guard for Your Second Coming to the world or to my life at death. Let me be prepared every day to come to meet You in eternity.*